REVISE FOR GERMAN GCSE

Listening and Speaking

Michael Buckby with John Pugh

Heinemann Educational Publishers,
Halley Court,
Jordan Hill,
Oxford OX2 8EJ

A division of Reed Educational & Professional Publishing Limited

OXFORD FLORENCE PRAGUE MADRID ATHENS MELBOURNE
AUCKLAND KUALA LUMPUR SINGAPORE TOKYO IBADAN NAIROBI
KAMPALA JOHANNESBURG GABORONE PORTSMOUTH NH (USA)
CHICAGO MEXICO CITY SAO PAOLO

© John Pugh 1997

First published 1997

00 99 98 97

10 9 8 7 6 5 4 3 2 1

A catalogue record is available for this book from the British Library on request.

ISBN 0 435 33267 8

Produced by Ken Vail Graphic Design, Cambridge

Illustrations by Julie Sailing-Free

Cover illustration by Vikki Liogier

Printed and bound in Edinburgh by Scotprint Ltd

Acknowledgements

The author and publishers would like to thank Michael Buckby and Kate Corney for their support and encouragement, and Marieke O'Connor for her painstaking editing.

The publishers would also like to thank the following for permission to reproduce copyright material:

London Examinations, a division of Edexcel Foundation; Midland Examining Group (MEG); Northern Examinations and Assessment Board (NEAB); Southern Examinations Group (SEG), Associated Examining Board; Welsh Joint Education Committee (WJEC).

Please note:

> Edexcel Foundation, London Examinations accepts no responsibility whatsoever for the accuracy or method of working in the answers given.
>
> MEG is not responsible for any third party copyright material used in their Specimen Papers.
>
> The NEAB is not responsible for worked solutions to questions and/or commentaries on the questions or possible answers. They are the sole responsibility of the author and may not necessarily constitute the only possible solutions.
>
> Any answers or hints on answers are the sole responsibility of the author and have neither been provided nor approved by SEG.

Every effort has been made to contact copyright holders of material in this book. Any omissions will be rectified in subsequent printings if notice is given to the publishers.

Contents

Introduction 5
Preparing for your GCSE 6

Listening

How to prepare for your listening exam 7

Part 1 (Foundation) 10
A Everyday activities 10
B Personal and social life 15
C The world around us 20
D The world of work 24
E The international world 27

Part 2 (Foundation/Higher) 29
A Everyday activities 29
B Personal and social life 30
C The world around us 33
D The world of work 35
E The international world 38

Part 3 (Higher) 40
A Everyday activities 40
B Personal and social life 43
C The world around us 46
D The world of work 49
E The international world 52

Solutions 106
Transcript 111

Speaking

How to prepare for your speaking exam 55

Area A Everyday activities 58
Area B Personal and social life 75
Practising under exam conditions 83
Area C The world around us 84
Area D The world of work 91
Practising under exam conditions 95
Area E The international world 97
Presentation
(Foundation and higher) 104
Solutions 123

If you are entered for Foundation Tier (aiming at Grades C to G) you need to work only on Parts 1 and 2 of this book, for listening. If you are entered for Higher Tier (aiming at Grades A* to C) you need to work on Parts 2 and 3 only, for listening.

If you are entered for Foundation Tier (aiming at Grades C to G), you need to practise only the activities marked Foundation and Foundation/Higher of this book, for speaking. If you are entered for Higher Tier (aiming at Grades A* to C) you need to practise only the activities marked Foundation/Higher and Higher.

By working on the two appropriate sections you will cover each topic at least once.

Introduction

Revise for German Listening and Speaking will show you how to get the best possible marks in the listening and speaking papers of your exam. By working through this book you will encounter all the different question types used by the GCSE examination boards and you will work on questions from all the different Areas of Experience, so you will be fully prepared. Each question is accompanied by helpful advice on what examiners are looking for and useful tips on exam technique. For the speaking questions model answers are given.

There is an introduction for the listening section of this book (page 7) and for the speaking section (page 55). You should read the tips there before you start working on the questions.

Listening

The listening section is divided into three parts:

Part 1   Questions at Foundation level (Grades E, F and G)
Part 2   Questions at Foundation/Higher level (Grades C and D)
Part 3   Questions at Higher level (Grades A*, A and B)

If you are entered for Foundation Tier (aiming at Grades C to G) you need to work on Parts 1 and 2 only. If you are entered for Higher Tier (aiming at Grades A* to C) you need to work on Parts 2 and 3 only.

In each Part the questions are presented by Area of Experience. By working on the two appropriate sections you will cover each topic at least once.

Speaking

The speaking section is not divided into Parts. Simply work through the section and choose the questions at the appropriate level (either Foundation and Foundation/Higher or Foundation/Higher and Higher).

The section is organised by Area of Experience. For each topic there is either a rôle-play question or conversation questions, or both, depending on the type of questions which come up in the examination. At the end of the section there is advice on preparing for a presentation. Check with your teacher whether you will have to give a presentation in the speaking exam.

The symbol indicates that you can listen to the rôle-play or the conversation on tape.

Preparing for your GCSE

One very useful way to prepare for your GCSE exam is to find out exactly what you need to know, understand and do. To do this, get hold of a syllabus and sample exam papers from the Exam Board (see addresses below) whose exam you are taking.

Write a letter like this to the Secretary of your Board, saying the following.

```
Dear Madam/Sir,

Could you please send me a copy of your
German GCSE syllabus (Long/Short* course) and
a sample paper. Thank you in advance.

Yours faithfully,
```

* Ask for the Long or Short course, whichever you are entered for.

Below are the addresses of all the GCSE Boards. With their permission, this book shows how to answer typical questions set by the Boards in their listening and speaking tests.

London Examinations,
Edexcel Foundation,
Stewart House,
32 Russell Square,
London WC1B 5DN

Midland Examination Group
(MEG), Syndicate Buildings,
1 Hills Road,
Cambridge CB1 2EU

Northern Examinations and
Assessment Board (NEAB),
31–33 Springfield Avenue,
Harrogate,
North Yorkshire HG1 2HW

Southern Examinations
Group (SEG),
Publications Dept.,
Stag Hill House,
Guildford,
Surrey GU2 5XJ

Welsh Joint Education
Committee (WJEC),
245 Western Avenue,
Cardiff CG5 2YX

Northern Ireland Schools
Examinations Council (NISEC),
29 Clarendon Road,
Belfast BT1 3BG

How to prepare for your listening exam

This book will show you how to get the best possible grade in your GCSE exam. As you work through it, you will learn how to answer the sorts of questions put by all the Exam Boards. You will also find out what the examiners are looking for and how to score top marks.

- The first thing to learn is exactly what you need to be able to do in your listening test to earn a Grade C. This is what you have to show the examiners you can do:
  - **Identify and note main points, and extract details and points of view,** from German spoken at normal speed. The German you hear will include narratives and future events. What you hear will cover a variety of topics and include familiar language in unfamiliar contexts.

- This is what you have to learn to do, in addition, to earn a Grade A* in listening:
  - **Understand gist and identify main points and details** in a variety of types of authentic spoken German.
  - **Recognise points of view, attitudes and emotions and draw conclusions** from what you hear.

Try to keep these points in mind as you work on this book and cassette, and as you listen to other things in German at school and at home. The best way to become really good at listening to German is to do a lot of it over several months – so practise listening as much as you can.

How to use the book and cassette

It is a fact that most people score less well at listening in GCSE than in any other skill! You don't need to be one of those people. You can learn from this book and cassette how to convince the examiners who mark your exam that you can do what they want you to do.

1   It is a huge help if you have learnt the words you will hear, and you can easily learn most of them in advance of the exam. Before you work on a topic, work first on the vocabulary for that topic in *GCSE German Vocabulary* (Heinemann).

    If, as you listen, you come across words you have not learnt, write them down and learn them. You will see that certain words come up time and again in listening tests. If you know these words you will score much higher marks. An example of this is numbers, so make sure that you really learn your German numbers: this alone could improve your result by a grade.

2   When you start on this book and cassette, you should not expect your listening skills to be as good as they will be by the time you have finished. So be patient with yourself and don't be discouraged! Here are some of the activities you can do to help you to improve. Do try them – they will really work:

- Stop the cassette as often as you need to. Play the German several times, as many times as you need to in order to feel really comfortable with it. Don't worry if you don't understand some German the first time you hear it.

- As your confidence builds up, you can sometimes let the cassette run on: you will often understand better when you listen to more of the recording.

- When you start on the book and cassette you will help yourself a lot if you also use the transcripts (see pages 111–122). Here are four steps for you. Start with **a** and then work up to **b**, **c** and **d** as you progress:

a   The first time you listen to the recording, follow the transcript as you listen. This helps to build important links between how words look and how they sound. You can look up in a dictionary any words you can't understand. Then listen to the recording again, without looking at the transcript. It should help your confidence a lot to see how much you can now understand!

b   When you feel ready, try listening to recordings without the transcript. Answer as many questions in the book as you can. Then read the transcript as you listen again and try again to answer the questions. Make a note of any important words or phrases which you didn't understand and then learn them. Then listen again, without the transcript, to be sure that you can now understand these words when you hear them.

c   When you feel more confident, listen to the recordings without the transcript and answer all the questions. Listen to the recordings two or three times if it helps. Next, read the transcript without listening to the recording and see if that helps you with any of the questions. Then go back to the questions and listen to the recording again, trying to answer all of them, without looking back at the transcript.

d   Finally, try working on questions as you will have to in your exam. Begin by reading the questions and using them to focus your mind on what you need to listen for. Play the recording once and then write, with a pencil, any answers you have found. Look again at the questions to focus your mind and then listen to the recording again. Write all your answers with a pen.

Now check your answers with the Solutions, at the back of the book. If you have any problems, look at the transcript and try to work out where you went wrong and how to get all the answers right. Then try again, looking at the questions and listening to the recording without the transcript. Keep on until you can answer all the questions easily. You will then be ready to score very high marks in your exam!

3. You can improve your learning by using a variety of exercises. Changing from one to another every now and then will help maintain your interest and develop different skills. Here are some ideas which will work well:

- Photocopy a transcript which you have worked on and cover up, or blank out, some words. Don't have too many gaps – no more than one per line. Then listen again to the recording and try to write in the missing words.

- Study a short transcript (or short extract from a longer transcript: don't try this with long texts!) and try to learn it. Then put the book away and listen to the recording. As you listen, write down the whole text, then compare what you have written with the transcript. Carry on until you can listen and write it perfectly. It will also help your learning if you leave a time gap between studying the transcript and trying to write it while you listen. Try increasing the gap, gradually, to a week or so.

- As you work with a recording and become familiar with it, pause it from time to time and try to say, or write, what comes next. Then play on and see how accurate you were.

- If you have had problems picking out, or understanding, some key words or phrases in a recording, write these down. Then listen to the recording again and tick them as soon as you hear them.

- Look at the English equivalents you have written for any German expressions you have heard in a recording and want to learn. Then listen, alone or with some friends, and try to spot the German equivalents as you hear them.

4. Start your preparations for the exam in good time, a year before if you can. Then do a little and often. Two sessions a week of half an hour each would be an excellent way to prepare for success. You can work your way through the three books in this series *(Revise for German GCSE Reading and Writing, Revise for German GCSE Listening and Speaking, GCSE German Vocabulary)* in that time. This will teach you the language, the skills and the exam techniques you need to achieve the best possible grade.

Good luck with your preparation and your exams!

Listening: Part 1

In Part 1, you can learn how to do most of what you need to get a grade C:

- **Identify and note main points** from German, spoken at normal speed.

A Everyday activities

1 School

> ◆ Give yourself one minute to read the question. Make sure you understand it. The question tells you what to listen for. To gain four marks you have to listen for the four school subjects for the rest of the day.
>
> ◆ Listen to the recording to try to find the answers. Note them in pencil.
>
> ◆ Listen to the recording again as many times as you need to. Use this to check your answers or to find them if you missed them the first time.
>
> ◆ Write your answers with a pen. You must write four subjects. If you are not sure, guess – a gap will never score a mark but an intelligent guess might!

Du gehst mit deinem deutschen Freund in die Schule. Was für Fächer hast du heute? Schreib die Fächer für A–D. [4 marks]

	1. Stunde	2. Stunde	3. Stunde	4. Stunde	5. Stunde	6. Stunde
Montag	Mathe	Biologie	Physik	Mathe	Englisch	frei
Dienstag	Deutsch	Englisch	A	B	C	D

© Northern Examinations and Assessment Board 1996

(Solution: page 106)

Listening
Part 1

2 Home Life

- As always, begin by reading the question very carefully. Make sure you understand it and use the information there to help you to know what to listen for.

- For this question you need to write two of your answers in German. There are four marks for Number 1 and one each for Numbers 2 and 3.

- Remember that you only need to write a simple answer and that as long as your German can be recognised to be correct you will get the mark. To be safe, though, it does pay to be as accurate as possible with your spelling.

1 Was macht der Junge, um seinen Eltern zu helfen?
   Schreib die vier richtigen Buchstaben.

   a das Auto waschen   e den Tisch decken
   b abwaschen   f einkaufen
   c sein Zimmer aufräumen   g im Garten arbeiten
   d die Fenster putzen   h den Mülleimer raustragen   [4]

2 Warum geht er gern einkaufen?
   Er kauft sich …   [1]

3 Wieviel Taschengeld bekommt der Junge?
   Er bekommt DM … .   [1]

(Solution: page 106)   [6 marks]

3 Health and Fitness

- Read the questions and use them to help you know what to listen for.

- In Number 1 the pictures will also help you: they show that it is either a headache and/or a temperature, stomach-ache, toothache or earache. Think of the German word for head, stomach etc. And listen to find out which it is.

- For Number 2, count the number of days or weeks.

- In Number 3, read the alternative answers carefully. Listen again to check your answers. Be sure to choose only one answer – any doubt in the marker's mind about your choice means no mark for you!

Listening
Part 1

BEIM ARZT

1 Was hat sie? Wähl das richtige Bild (A–D).

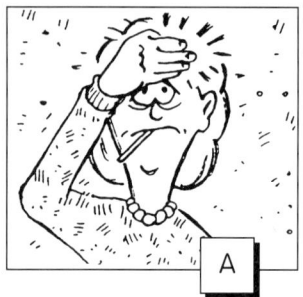 A
 B
 C
 D

2 Seit wann hat sie das? Wähl den richtigen Kalender (A–D).

3 Was macht der Arzt? Wähl die richtige Antwort (A–D).

   A Er verschreibt etwas.

   B Sie verschreibt etwas.

   C Er gibt ihr Tabletten.

   D Er schreibt einen Brief.

[3 marks]

(Solution: page 106)   © Welsh Joint Education Committee 1995

Listening
Part 1

4 Food

▶ You are now ready to work on several questions together, one of which is rather long – good practice for your exam! Remember what you have learnt about tackling each question:
1. Use the question to help you know what to listen for.
2. Listen once and note the answers in pencil.
3. Listen again to check your answers and fill in any gaps. Then write your answers with a pen.

▶ In **a** and **b** you simply have to choose the correct drink or snack.

▶ In **c**, choose the correct bill for the order given. Remember the advice you were given about knowing your numbers thoroughly – they have a habit of cropping up!

IM CAFÉ

Beispiel: Was trinkt deine Freundin? Schreib A, B oder C. *B* [3 marks]

a Was trinkt dein Freund? Schreib A, B oder C.

b Was möchte er noch? Schreib A, B oder C.

c Welche Rechnung ist richtig? Schreib A, B oder C.

A Café Dorfwirt	B Café Dorfwirt	C Café Dorfwirt
1,20	2,20	6,00
2,70	3,70	10,00
1,30	9,30	5,00
		4,00
DM 5,20	DM 15,20	DM 25,00

© London Examinations, a division of Edexcel Foundation 1996

(Solution: page 106)

Listening
Part 1

5 Food

- For question 5 the recording is much longer. There are 12 marks to gain by correctly identifying who had what to eat.

- Once again, help yourself by working out the words for as many of the pictures as you can. If necessary, give yourself extra pauses while playing the recording to help you think it through.

- Concentrate on the food items you hear, as well as the speaker. To make it easier for you, the examiner has put the pictures in the order you will hear each item. To answer, write the person's initial for each numbered picture.

Was ißt man in Deutschland? Was ißt man in England? Wer hat was gegessen? Schreib die Zahlen 1–12 und C (Christian), H (Heinz) oder S (Steffi) daneben.

[12 marks]

(Solution: page 106)

© SEG Specimen Papers 1997

Listening
Part 1

B Personal and social life

6 Self, family and friends

◘ Many words in German look very similar to their English equivalents but sound very different. One good technique to help you to understand words like these is to practise writing them down when you hear them. This way you link the sound and the written form of the word and recognise it more easily. Practise this technique with the words below. Listen to the recording and find the letter of the correct word from this jumbled list. Say each word several times as you read it.

A: Adresse   F: England
B: Station   G: Garage
C: Finger   H: Hand
D: Supermarkt   I: Minute
E: Religion   J: Student

◘ Much of the material in this section covers work you did very early on in your German course and is therefore relatively straightforward. Nonetheless, read each question very carefully to anticipate the information needed and listen at least twice to check your answers.

◘ You can see how much information to give by looking at the marks for each section. Most exam boards allow you to use a dictionary for a few minutes before the listening test. You may need to look up an occasional word such as *Beruf* in the second question during the preparation period. You have to be very careful not to rely too much on the dictionary, but used wisely it is a useful tool.

◘ This question spells out the names for you. It's a good idea to revise the German alphabet sounds as you may find you need them for your speaking exam.

Eine Kassette von einer neuen Brieffreundin. Schreib die Antworten auf deutsch.

a Name, Alter, Wohnort.   [3]
b Geschwister, Hobbys, Haustier.   [4]

                                                                [7 marks]

(Solution: page 106)   © Northern Examinations and Assessment Board 1996

Listening
Part 1

7 Self, family and friends

> The next question deals with a description of a German boy. Study the pictures carefully and try to think of some German words you are likely to hear. Pick out the differences.

You listen to a German boy describing what he looks like. What does he look like? Write A, B, C or D. [1 mark]

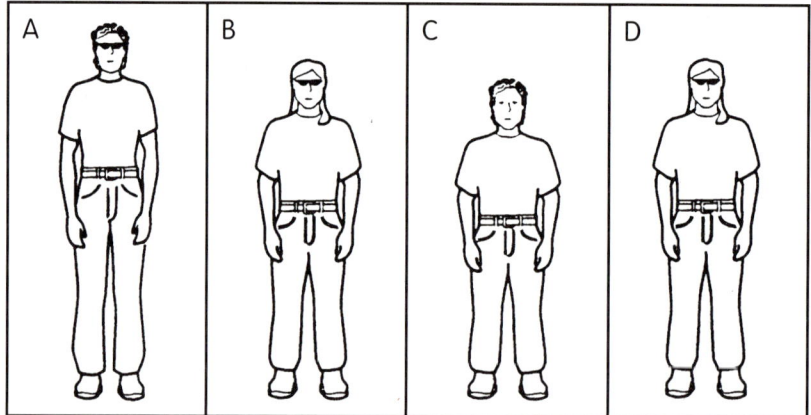

© MEG Specimen Papers 1997/8

(Solution: page 106)

8 Leisure and entertainment

> The (3) tells you that there are three marks available for this question. You will need to give the type of film, the day and the time it starts. So, rehearse all the German words you know for types of film, the days of the week and how to express the time in German.

> Remember that the time in Germany is usually given in the 24 hour clock. It doesn't matter which you use in your answer, but don't confuse the two by answering 'eight o'clock' for *achtzehn Uhr* (six o' clock). Remember you take away 12 to get to the 12 hour clock.

> Another point to remember is the use of *halb* in German. Think of it as 'half **to** the hour'. So *halb neun* is 'halfway to nine' or as we say 'half past eight'.

IM KINO

Dein Freund ruft beim Kino Capitol an. Schreib die drei Antworten für a, b und c. **Beispiel**: Film   André

   a Filmkategorie   **b** Tag   **c** Uhrzeit   [3 marks]

© London Examinations, a division of Edexcel Foundation 1996

(Solution: page 106)

9 Free time, holidays and special occasions

- In your exam you will be expected to answer several questions in the time allowed. The questions below will help prepare you. Give yourself three minutes to study all five questions and the visuals.

- Make absolutely sure that you understand all the questions. If you need to, look up any words you don't know in the dictionary – but don't go over three minutes.

- Use the questions and the visuals to work out what the answer will probably sound like – this will help you to hear it on the recording. For example, you can look at the first question and work out that the key words for your answer will come from:

    A: fernsehen
    B: schwimmen
    C: kochen
    D: reiten
    E: zu Partys gehen
    F: Hockey spielen
    G: lesen
    H: Fahrrad fahren

- Read the instructions carefully and note that only five boxes are to be chosen. If you tick more than five, marks will be deducted even if you have included all five correct choices! Be careful, there are also a couple of hobbies on the recording which are not illustrated.

1 Jetzt spricht Sabine über ihre Hobbys. Schauen Sie sich die Bilder an. Und jetzt hören Sie zu. Schreiben Sie **nur** fünf Buchstaben. [5 marks]

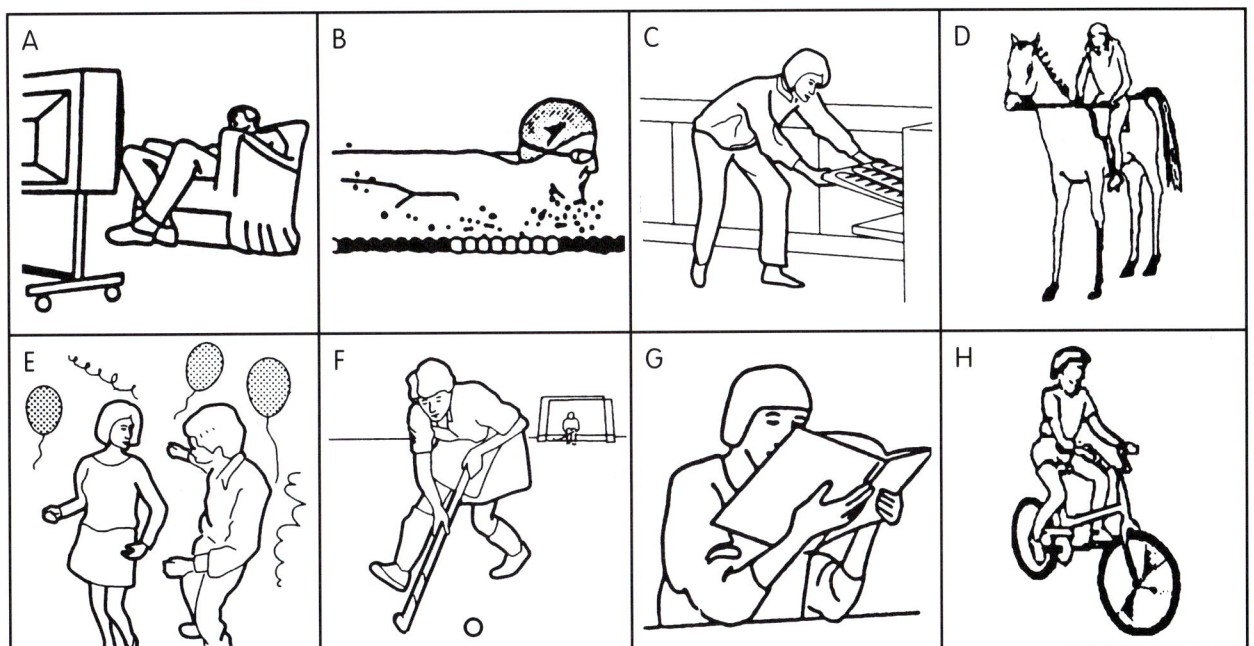

© MEG Specimen Papers 1997/8

Listening
Part 1

2 You hear two teenagers talking about their pocket money. What does the boy spend his money on? Write down the correct letter. [1 mark]

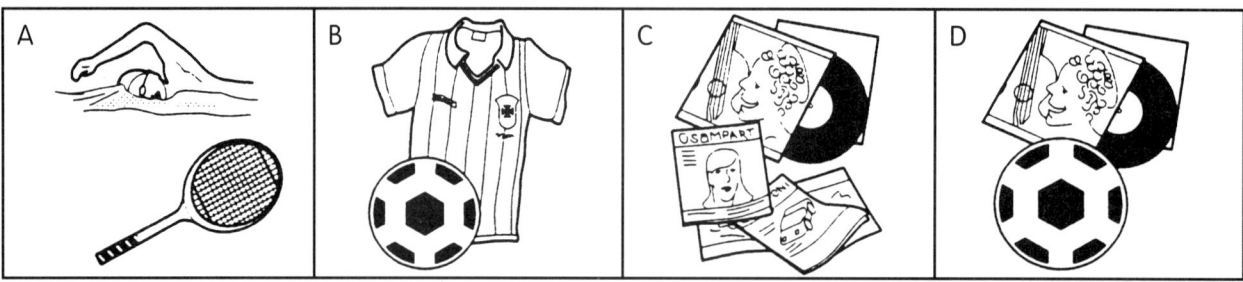

© MEG Specimen Papers 1997/8

3 Schreib den richtigen Buchstaben.
Beispiel: Was macht Peter gern? B und D

Peter	 A	 B	 C	 D
Sabine	E	F	G	H

  a Was macht Peter nicht gern? [1]
  b Was macht Sabine gern? [2]
  c Was macht Sabine nicht gern? [1]

[4 marks]

© Northern Examinations and Assessment Board 1996

4 Was will Jan am Wochenende machen? Schreib Freitag, Samstag oder Sonntag für a, b und c.

  a am Computer spielen
  b tanzen gehen
  c fernsehen [3 marks]

© London Examinations, a division of Edexcel Foundation 1996

5 Welche Aktivitäten wollen Ina, Dieter und Ulrike am Wochenende machen? Schreib drei Aktivitäten.

  a Ina   **b** Dieter   **c** Ulrike   [3 marks]

© Northern Examinations and Assessment Board 1996

[20 marks]

(Solutions: page 107)

Listening
Part 1

10 Arranging a meeting or activity

- The secret to success in your listening exam is your preparation **before** listening to a recording. Use what you have learnt to prepare yourself before you listen.

- If you need a reminder of what to do, look back at page 8.

- Getting the right answer often depends on hearing and understanding one or two key words for each question. Before you try answering the questions below, listen and match the words on the recording with the key words below.

  A: am Computer spielen   D: fernsehen

  B: vier Uhr   E: Fußballspiel

  C: wandern   F: treffen

- A big advantage of learning to write down the key words you hear, is that you may be able to look up in a dictionary any you can't understand. If you write the words next to the question on the exam paper, you may be able to look them up in a dictionary at the end and then write your answers. Practise doing this as it could earn you several extra marks in your exam – marks which could take you a grade higher.

1 Du bist bei deinem Brieffreund, der nicht zu Hause ist. Das Telefon klingelt. Schreib den Satz ohne Lücken!

Peter, du sollst Anna um … Uhr im … treffen. [2 marks]

© Welsh Joint Education Committee 1995

2 Es ist jetzt 17.30 Uhr. Du willst den Film „Forrest Gump" sehen. Schreib die Antworten aus.

  a Die nächste Vorstellung von „Forrest Gump" beginnt um …

  b Für dich als Erwachsene kostet es DM …

  c Dein Freund ist 18 Jahre alt, und er hat keine Arbeit. Seine Eintrittskarte kostet DM …   [3 marks]

© Northern Examinations and Assessment Board 1996

3 Two boys are planning an activity. Listen carefully and answer these three questions **in English**.

  a What does Bruno invite Dieter to do?

  b Why can't Dieter meet Bruno today?

  c What time will they meet on Tuesday?   [3 marks]

[8 marks]

(Solutions: page 106)

Listening
Part 1

C The world around us

11 Home town, local environment and customs

- Use the techniques you have learnt to prepare for and answer these questions.

- Remember that you may have to listen to quite a lot of German before you have the information you need to answer a question. You are more likely to be able to pick out the correct answer if you have prepared yourself for the question **before** you listen to the recording.

- In this question you are required to read a series of statements and decide whether they are true or false after listening to the recording. Clearly, careful preparation will make a great difference.

- Don't expect to hear the same words in the recording as you see on the page – the examiner is testing your overall understanding, not just certain words. In **d** you read *Es hat ein Kino*. One letter can change the meaning entirely and you need to listen carefully to the German to catch it – *Es hat **kein** Kino*.

- You may want to look up the odd word such as *sehenswert* in your dictionary if you can't remember it.

Zwei Deutsche sprechen über Kappeldorf, eine Stadt in der Nähe von Osnabrück.

Wenn die Aussage richtig ist, schreiben Sie ein **R** (richtig).
Wenn die Aussage falsch ist, schreiben Sie ein **F** (falsch).

Beispiel: Kappeldorf ist eine Stadt.   R

Lesen Sie die Fragen a–g. Und jetzt hören Sie zu.

   a Kappeldorf ist 900 Jahre alt.
   b Das Schloß ist sehenswert.
   c Kappeldorf steht mitten im Wald.
   d Es hat ein Kino.
   e Man kann Lebensmittel in Kappeldorf kaufen.
   f Man kann Kleidung in Kappeldorf kaufen.
   g Inge fährt mit der Straßenbahn nach Osnabrück. [7 marks]

(Solution: page 106) © MEG Specimen Papers 1997/8

12 Finding the way

Before you start the questions in this section, practise linking spoken and written forms with these words.

A: *links*
B: *rechts*
C: *geradeaus*
D: *gegenüber*
E: *bis zur Ampel*
F: *an der Kreuzung*
G: *über die Brücke*
H: *um die Ecke*
I: *an der Post vorbei*
J: *zu Fuß*

1 Wo ist das Kaufhaus? Was ist richtig? A, B, C oder D? [1 mark]

Beispiel: Wo ist die Post? D

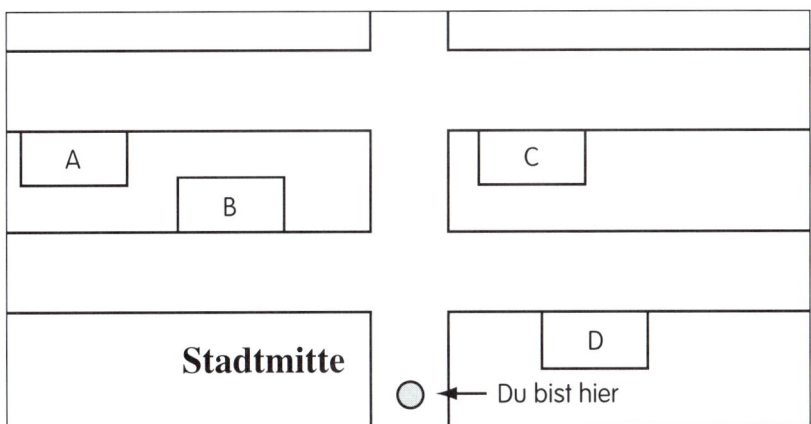

© London Examinations, a division of Edexcel Foundation 1996

2 Your parents have lost their way. They are given directions to the car park. Where is the car park? Write A, B, C or D. [1 mark]

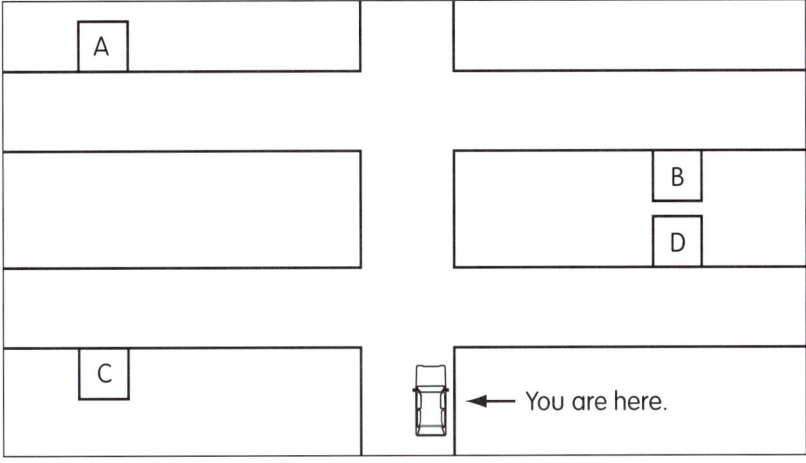

© MEG Specimen Papers 1997/8

(Solutions: page 106)

Listening
Part 1

13 Shopping

> ◘ Begin, as usual, by making sure you understand the questions and using them to help you prepare to listen and to answer. Use the techniques you know for doing this.
>
> ◘ In shopping situations you will find that numbers and quantities play an important role. Make some time to revise your numbers up to 100.
>
> ◘ You have to listen carefully to distinguish between *vierzehn* and *fünfzehn* with some German speakers. Don't fall into the trap of mixing up numbers ending in *-zehn* and *-zig* – it makes a great difference!

1 You go shopping with the mother of your German penfriend. What is she buying? Write A, B, C or D. [1 mark]

© MEG Specimen Papers 1997/8

2 IM KAUFHAUS

In welchen Stock gehst du? Schreib 1, 2, 3 oder 4.

Beispiel: Du willst ein Buch kaufen. **2**

Du willst einen Fußball kaufen. [1 mark]

© London Examinations, a division of Edexcel Foundation 1996

3 You are listening to the radio and hear a recipe for a cake. How much of each of the following ingredients do you need to make it?

Example: flour   200g

a eggs

b butter

c apples

d sugar [4 marks]

© London Examinations, a division of Edexcel Foundation 1996

(Solutions: page 106)

14 Getting around

◆ It would be a good idea now to look back over the advice you were given in Sections A, B and C. Read it all again and make sure you know all there is to know about:
1 using the questions and pictures to prepare before you listen;
2 picking out and understanding the key words in the recordings which you need for your answers;
3 checking that you have listened accurately and written your answers accurately.

◆ Practice using these techniques as you prepare to answer and then complete these six questions. Listen to the recording as many times as you need to.

1 You want to go to the swimming pool and somebody tells you which tram to take. Write the correct number of the tram.

   A 5   **B** 10   **C** 15   **D** 25   [1 mark]

   © MEG Specimen Papers 1997/8

2 Wann kommt der nächste Bus? Schreib A, B oder C. [1 mark]

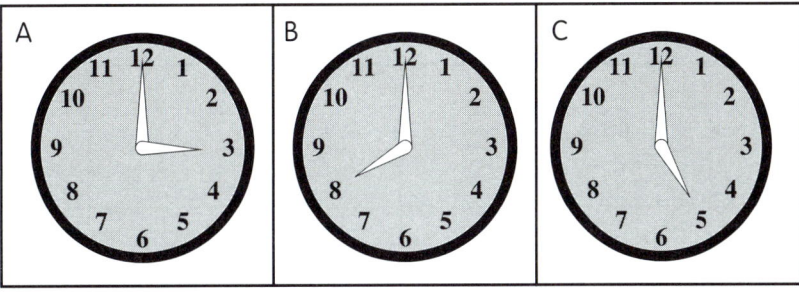

© London Examinations, a division of Edexcel Foundation 1996

3 Von welchem Gleis fährt der Zug ab? Schreib A, B oder C.

   A Gleis 5   **B** Gleis 15   **C** Gleis 10   [1 mark]

   © London Examinations, a division of Edexcel Foundation 1996

4 Was kostet eine Karte? Die Antwort ist DM … [1 mark]

   © London Examinations, a division of Edexcel Foundation 1996

5 Schreiben Sie die Sätze ohne Lücken.
   Lesen Sie die Sätze **a – d**. Und jetzt hören Sie zu.

   Beispiel: Die Frau muß … fahren. *Die Frau muß zum Flughafen fahren.*

   a Die Maschine fliegt … ab.   **c** Die Frau sagt, ein Taxi ist …
   b Die Bahn ist …   **d** Die Frau fährt … zum Flughafen. [4 marks]

   © MEG Specimen Papers 1997/8

(Solutions: page 106)

Listening Part 1

D The world of work

15 Education and training

◆ In this question you will hear five young people talking about their career hopes. You must study the pictures carefully and decide which jobs match each speaker. The names have been written out for you and an example is shown. Before you listen to the recording, prepare in the usual way by thinking of the German word for each job.

◆ Listen carefully to the whole speech before writing your answer, because some of the speakers mention jobs which they don't want to do. If you find this question difficult, read the script on page 113 and then listen again while you read.

AUF DEM ARBEITSAMT

Was für einen Beruf wollen Katja, Jens, Jörg, Bärbel und Peter? Schreib den richtigen Buchstaben für jeden Namen.

Beispiel: Katja C

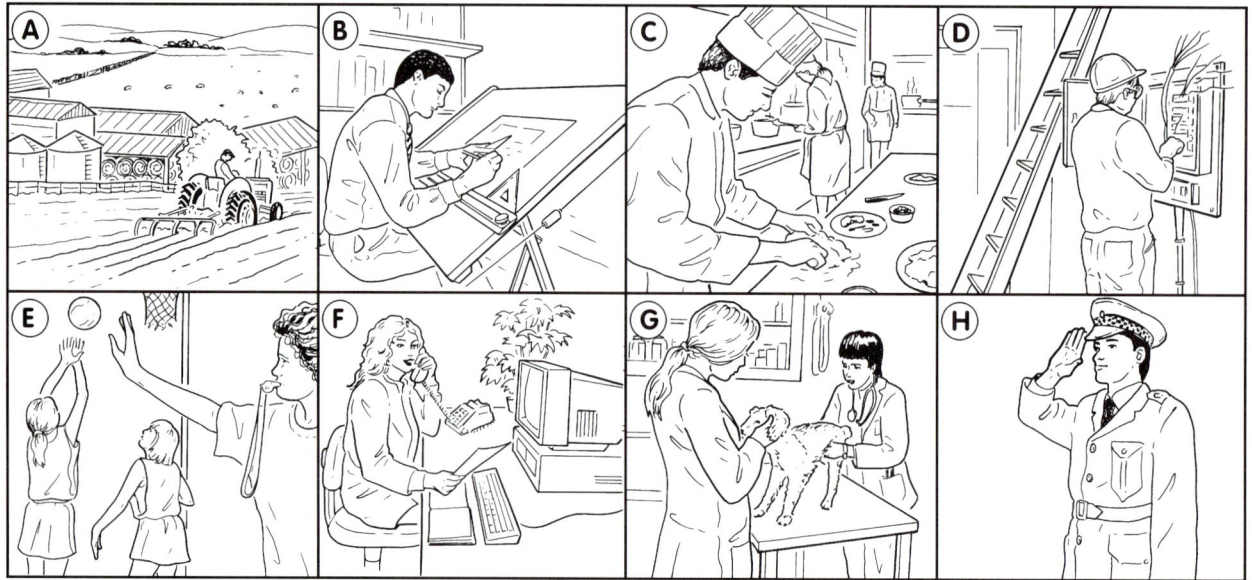

1 Jens
2 Jörg
3 Bärbel
4 Peter

[4 marks]

(Solutions: page 106)   © Northern Examinations and Assessment Board 1996

16 Careers and employment

⟡ The first question in this part is good practice for matching spoken and written forms. You are asked to listen to a job interview and to check off on the list those questions which actually occur in the interview.

⟡ Of course, not only are some of the questions on the list not asked, but some are only slightly different from the one you read on the page. Note there are eight marks and therefore eight correct questions. You will lose marks if you include any extra guesses!

1 Hör ein Gespräch zwischen einem deutschen Arbeitgeber und Mr Clarke aus England an. Schreib die Buchstaben von den Fragen, die du in dem Gespräch gehört hast. [8 marks]

A Haben Sie eine gute Reise gehabt?
B Ist Liverpool eine große Stadt?
C Woher kommen Sie?
D Wo liegt Liverpool?
E Wo liegt Warrington?
F Spielen Sie Fußball?
G Sehen Sie sich viele Fußballspiele an?
H Haben Sie auch andere Interessen?
I Haben Sie einen Samstagsjob?
J Was machen Sie samstags?
K Was machen Sie am Samstag?
L Was für eine Schule besuchen Sie?
M Was sind Ihre Lieblingsfächer?
N Welche sind Ihre Leistungsfächer?
O Welche Fächer machen Sie gern?
P Seit wann lernen Sie Deutsch?
Q Ist Deutsch Ihr Lieblingsfach?
R Lernen Sie auch Französisch?
S Warum wollen Sie in Deutschland arbeiten?
T Warum wollen Sie hier arbeiten?

© SEG Specimen Papers 1997

2 HEIKE

a Was ist Heikes Vater von Beruf? Wähl A, B oder C. [1 mark]

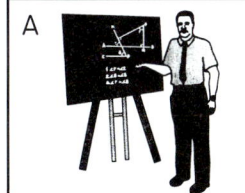  

b Wo arbeitet Heikes Mutter? Wähl A, B oder C.
   A Krankenhaus   B Restaurant   C Bank   [1 mark]

c Was möchte Heikes Bruder machen? Wähl A, B oder C. [1 mark]

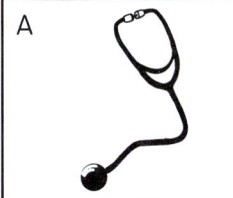  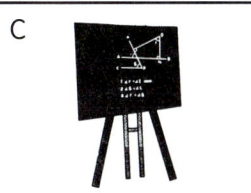

© London Examinations, a division of Edexcel Foundation 1996

(Solutions: page 106)

Listening
Part 1

17 Advertising and publicity

- These four radio advertisements are a kind of revision because they are about topics covered earlier in the book.

- There are no visual clues to help you, so listen carfully. Note that there is one mark for each answer, which means you write one piece of information.

You are listening to the radio when you hear four advertisements. Your English friend wants to know what is being advertised. Write a list of the four products. [4 marks]

© London Examinations, a division of Edexcel Foundation 1996

(Solution: page 107)

18 Communication

- This section of the syllabus is mainly about telephoning, so telephone numbers will often be used to test you.

- Spend some time revising your German numbers before you answer this question. Numbers often come up in speaking exams, so learning them thoroughly does two jobs for you.

- In this question the *Vorwahlnummer* is mentioned – this is the dialling code for a town or country. You need to get the full number right to get the mark, because, the examiner says, just one figure incorrect would give a wrong number.

Du hörst den Anrufbeantworter ab. Auf ihm ist eine Liste der Telefonnummern von Firmen und Büros in Koblenz. Der Chef hat nach diesen Nummern gefragt. Schreib die Nummern auf.

    a Vorwahl

    b Verkehrsbüro

    c Herr Schmidt (privat)

    d Freibad

    e Hotel Panorama

    f Firma Bock [6 marks]

© SEG Specimen Papers 1997/8

(Solution: page 107)

 The **international world**

19 Life in other countries and communities

> - This section of the syllabus deals simply with handling money in German-speaking countries.
> - This example has prices in German currency: the Mark and the Pfennig. You must also be familiar with the Swiss Franken and Rappen and the Austrian Schilling and Groschen. In each case there are 100 of the second smaller unit in the first one, i.e. 100 Rappen (Rp) = 1 Franken (Fr), 100 Groschen (g) = 1 Schilling (S) and, as you know, 100 Pfennig (Pf.) = 1 (Deutsche) Mark (DM).

You are shopping in the supermarket in Germany with your parents when you hear these special offers announced. Your parents want to know what the prices of the products are. Listen carefully and write down their prices.

    a tomatoes   **b** chocolate   **c** beer   **d** ice-cream   [4 marks]

(Solution: page 107)

20 Tourism

> - This exercise has no visuals to help you, but you have a series of very short questions which you can read carefully and prepare before you listen for the answers.
> - You can answer each question with just one word of German, if you like. For example, you need only write *Bus* for a means of transport rather than the more complete *mit dem Bus*. The main thing is to show your understanding in German. Notice that if *Bus* was the answer, you could lose a mark by forgetting your capital letter and writing the English word 'bus' by mistake!

Schreiben Sie die Antworten.
Lesen Sie die Fragen. Hören sie dann zu.

Beispiel: mitzunehmende Kleidung *Mantel*
    a Monat des Austausches   **e** Treffen – wo?
    b Wetter   **f** Besichtigungen, (i) und (ii)
    c Transport nach Deutschland   **g** Transport jeden Tag zur Schule [9 marks]
    d Treffen – wann?   **h** Aktivität am letzten Abend

© MEG Specimen Papers 1997/8

(Solution: page 107)

Listening
Part 1

21 Accommodation

- Remember everything you have learnt so far:
  1. Read the questions and look at the visuals **before** you listen,
  2. Listen to pick out the key words and key information,
  3. Write your answers,
  4. Check that you have listened and written accurately.

- This question about campsites is a good one to practise your techniques with.

CAMPINGPLÄTZE
Schreib die richtigen Buchstaben.
Beispiel: Was gibt es bei Camping Grünwald? B,C

A  B  C

D  E  F

   a Was gibt es bei Camping Hofbauer? [5]
   b Was gibt es bei Camping Mosel? [4]

[9 marks]

© Northern Examinations and Assessment Board 1996

(Solution: page 107)

22 The wider world

- The names of countries and nationalities are often easy to recognise when you see them written down but less obvious when you hear them.

- Before trying the exam question, sharpen your word recognition skills by listening to this recording of words to do with countries and nationalities. Match up the number of the word you hear with the correct letter from the list below.

- It is also a good exercise for revising some vocabulary.
  A: *Schottland*   E: *Italien*   H: *USA*
  B: *Amerikaner*   F: *England*   I: *Dänemark*
  C: *Irland*   G: *Afrika*   J: *Belgien*
  D: *Spanisch*

You hear three holiday adverts on the radio. Note down in **English** which country can be visited and add one other detail, for each of the three adverts, for a friend who is going on holiday soon. [6 marks]

© London Examinations, a division of Edexcel Foundation 1996

(Solution: page 107)

Listening: Part 2

In Part 2 you can learn how to do what you need to earn a grade C:
- **Identify and note main points** from German, spoken at normal speed.
- **Extract details and points of view** from German, spoken at normal speed.
- The spoken tests will include **narratives and future events**.
- The tests also include **familiar language in unfamiliar contexts**.

A Everyday activities

1 School

- Give yourself two minutes to read the question and look up in a dictionary any key English words in the question which you do not know and which you expect to hear in the recording. The first part (Number 1), contains no problems of that sort, but in the second part, (Number 2), you may want to look up the words for 'mark' and 'essay'. Write down the German words beside the question. German pupils are graded differently from you and the best grade is 1. Do not exceed two minutes – that's all the time you would have in the exam.
- Listen to the recording for Number 1 and try to find the information you need. Note in pencil any answers you find.
- Listen to the recording again. This time try and find any answers you may have missed the first time and check the answers you already have.
- Now follow the same steps for Number 2.
- Finally check your answers and write them with a pen. Try to answer every question. If you are not sure – guess; a blank will never score a mark, but a guess might.

You will hear a conversation between three young people, Brigitte, Dieter and Inge. They are talking about life at school. You will hear the conversation in two parts and you will hear each part twice.

1 First read through questions a–c. Now listen to the first part of the conversation. Write the correct name: Brigitte, Dieter or Inge.
  - **a** Who is not good at maths?
  - **b** Who likes doing maths?
  - **c** Who enjoys games?

2 First read through questions d–e. Now listen to the second part of the conversation. Again, write the correct name: Brigitte, Dieter or Inge.
  - **d** Who gets good marks for essays?
  - **e** Who is looking forward to the holidays?

[5 marks]

(Solution: page 107)

Listening
Part 2

2 Home life

> ◆ Check the statements **a–n** below. They will help you to know what to listen for in the recording. For example, in
> **a** You are listening for information about getting up, or a time.
> **b** You will hear something about the time of year – a holiday, date or month.
> **c** You may hear a time or simply this sentence with the addition of *nicht*.
> **d** You are listening for her age.

Hör bitte den Text an. Du hörst Informationen über ein deutsches Mädchen. Welche Sätze sind richtig? Schreib die Buchstaben von den richtigen Sätzen (a–n).

a Nikki schläft gern lange.
b Sie hat jetzt Winterferien.
c Sie steht sofort auf.
d Sie ist elf Jahre alt.
e Sie hat einen Vogel.
f Sie hat einen Kanarienvogel.
g Die Eltern arbeiten im Büro.
h Sie frühstückt allein.
i Morgens ist sie nicht allein.
j Wenn das Wetter schön ist, frühstückt sie im Garten.
k Daniela ist ihre beste Freundin.
l Sie ist ihre Schulfreundin.
m Sie telefoniert nicht mit ihr.
n Am Nachmittag gehen sie an den Fluß.

[9 marks]

© SEG Specimen Papers 1997

(Solution: page 107)

B Personal and social life

3 Self, family and friends

> ◆ Give yourself one minute to read this question and look up any words you can't understand. Be selective – the two most likely to be needed are *Wohnsitz* and *Rennen*.
>
> ◆ Once again, this is a test of your knowledge of numbers. Before you start this exercise, listen to the spoken form of some numbers and practise matching them to the written forms below.
>
> A: *Neunundvierzig*   F: 458
> B: *Eintausendzweihundert*   G: 1944
> C: *Achtzehnhundertfünfundsiebzig* H: 2500
> D: *Hundertvierzig*   I: 1789
> E: *Neunzehnhundertzweiunddreißig* J: 1981

EIN INTERVIEW MIT MICHAEL SCHUMACHER

Schreib die richtigen Informationen für den Steckbrief.

a Alter **b** Wohnsitz **c** Hobby **d** Erstes Rennen [4 marks]

© London Examinations, a division of Edexcel Foundation 1996

(Solution: page 107)

Listening
Part 2

4 Free time, holidays and special occasions

◆ As you prepare for your listening exam, practise a technique which can earn you enough marks in most exams to take you a grade higher: if you hear a key word which you don't understand, try to write it down. When you **see** the word, you can often understand it better than when you **hear** it.

◆ To practise, link up the words below with the words on the recording. Do this before you try the exam question. You will hear the whole list twice, but you can repeat it more often if you need to.

A: *über Pferde*   D: *zur Zeit*

B: *Was liest du?*   E: *ein englisches Buch*

C: *die Umwelt*   F: *ein ganz tolles Buch*

◆ This exam question is actually easier to understand once you hear the recording, because the types of book illustrated in the question become clearer. There isn't much to read, so you have time to think of a few types of books that you know in German.

◆ As you listen, remember to write down key words in German that you do not immediately understand. If you still can't recognise the meaning, you may have time to look them up at the end of the examination and gain an extra mark.

Wer liest was? Wähl das richtige Buch. Für A–D, schreib den richtigen Namen hin: Jan, Anna, Sven oder Lotte.   [4 marks]

(Solution: page 107)

© London Examinations, a division of Edexcel Foundation 1996

Listening
Part 2

5 Arranging a meeting or activity

◆ You can be sure that you will need to understand the time in German at some point in your listening exam. Make a point of revising expressions of time and numbers up to sixty before trying this question. Don't forget *Viertel* and *halb*, especially the last one with its 'half **to** the hour' meaning.

◆ This question doesn't offer many clues when you read it, except that there are seven marks available. That suggests that a very detailed answer is called for, but doesn't mean that the information is long or complicated. An answer such as: 'Friday/morning/at 10.30.' could carry three marks.

◆ Use the other techniques available to you:

1. listen carefully the first time and note any answers in pencil;
2. note any key words you may need to look up if you don't recognise the written form;
3. listen a second time to complete your answers and to check them;
4. write out your answers in ink when you have checked them.

Your brother's German friend Peter rings. He asks you to pass on a message to your brother. Write down, in English, the message you are given. [7 marks]

© Northern Examinations and Assessment Board 1996

(Solution: page 107)

6 Arranging a meeting or activity

◆ Question 6 is easier to answer and you can work out what you will be listening for in advance. This question also practises some of the material in Section C, both *Finding the Way* and *Getting Around*.

Your friend phones. How do you get to the party? Write your notes **in English**.

a Means of transport
b Route number
c Get off at the
d Walk as far as the
e The house is
f Telephone number [6 marks]

© Welsh Joint Education Committee 1995

(Solution: page 107)

Listening
Part 2

7 Home town, local environment and customs

> This question tests your knowledge of weather vocabulary in German, as you can see. Use the visuals to help you prepare for listening. As you study the pictures, think of the German words you know for the weather in each one.

Du hörst den Wetterbericht im Radio. Wie ist das Wetter in Deutschland?
Schreib die Buchstaben des passenden Bildes zu a–d.

1 In Norddeutschland   3 Im Rheinland
2 Im Süden   4 Im Osten   [4 marks]

A	B	C	D	E	F
		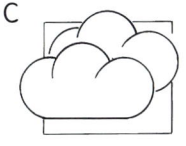	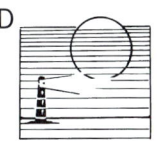	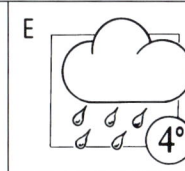	

(Solution: page 107)

8 Shopping

> Numbers, along with weights and measures, play an important role in exercises to do with shopping. Speaking tests are often set in shops too, so it's well worthwhile revising your weights and measures.
>
> *Das Kilo* = 1.000 *Gramm*
> *Das Pfund* = 500 *Gramm* (or *ein halbes Kilo*)
> *Ein halbes Pfund* = 250 *Gramm*
> (Our British pound is a little lighter at 454 grams, but the difference is slight as far as shopping is concerned.)

> Prepare yourself by working out the two numbers in German, to quickly recognise them during the recording.

Was ist heute im Sonderangebot?
Schreib zu A–E die fehlenden Artikel oder Preise.

Sonderangebot	Preis
Champignons	A
B	DM1.99
C	DM549
D	E

[5 marks]

(Solution: page 107)   © Northern Examinations and Assessment Board 1996

Listening
Part 2

9 Shopping

> This question requires answers in German. Read the question carefully, so that you know exactly what you are listening for. Note the German key words in pencil, as you have practised, when you listen to the recording. You only need to write very short answers, often just one or two words. Don't get anxious about spelling, but be as careful as you can. Showing that you have understood the text and the questions is the most important thing. After listening a second time, write your answers with a pen.

Die Chefin besucht die Firma Müller in Deutschland und möchte Geschenke mitnehmen. Du hörst gleich ein Telefongespräch zwischen der Sekretärin der Chefin in England und der Sekretärin des Chefs in Deutschland.

Du sollst schreiben:
– was für ein Geschenk jeder bekommt;
– weitere Informationen darüber (z.B. warum).

    a Herr Müller   **c** Herr Krause

    b Frau Meyer   **d** Frau Decker   [12 marks]

© SEG Specimen Papers 1997

(Solution: page 108)

10 Public services

> In this question you must read the three statements very carefully before listening to the recording. You may need to look up a word before listening to the recording, but remember you don't have long.

> Practise using your dictionary with this question before you listen. Choose three or four words from the three statements and look them up in your dictionary, as quickly as possible, noting the meanings in pencil on your answer paper. Time yourself, and don't go over two minutes. You'll see how few words you will be able to look up in a dictionary in the exam – concentrate rather on learning your vocabulary regularly and keep the dictionary for special cases only.

IM FUNDBÜRO

Richtig oder falsch? Schreib **R** oder **F** für 1–3.

    1 Sie hat ihren Koffer verloren.

    2 Sie hat den Rucksack im Zug liegenlassen.

    3 Sie muß morgen beim Fundbüro anrufen.   [3 marks]

© London Examinations, a division of Edexcel Foundation 1996

(Solution: page 108)

Listening
Part 2

D The world of work

- Some of the vocabulary in this section of the syllabus can be rather technical or complicated. German words tend to get longer, the more specific the meaning is. The words get longer because German speakers join shorter words to make longer ones. Words such as *Krankenschwester* and *Zahnarzt* are each made up of two words. Try to break longer words down into separate parts – it may help you to guess the meaning. Practise with this short list of examples:

  1 *Herbergsvater*
  2 *Arbeitsstelle*
  3 *Hausfrau*
  4 *Mathematiklehrerin*
  5 *Arbeitstag*
  6 *Öffnungszeiten*
  7 *Arbeitspraktikum*
  8 *Fahrtkosten*
  9 *Lastwagenmechaniker*
  10 *Zahnarzthelferin*

11 Education and training

- This question requires careful preparation. You have to understand the instructions and six questions before you start to listen.

- You will find it easier if you listen to each person twice and write an answer in pencil, before going on to the next speaker.

- When you have got to the end, repeat the whole recording once more to check your answers before writing them with a pen.

Schreiben Sie für jeden Schüler oder für jede Schülerin den Buchstaben, der am besten paßt.

A Wer möchte so bald wie möglich mehr Geld haben?
B Wer möchte sogar nach der Schulzeit weiterstudieren?
C Wer möchte in einer Werkstatt arbeiten?
D Wer möchte für eine Zeitung arbeiten?
E Wer möchte im Familienbetrieb arbeiten?
F Wer möchte sich für einen medizinischen Beruf ausbilden lassen?

1 Klaus
2 Martina
3 Ulrike
4 Manfred
5 Karl
6 Reinhard

[6 marks]

(Solution: page 108)

© MEG Specimen Papers 1997/8

Listening Part 2

12 Education and training

- In this question Petra is talking about her *Lehre* (apprenticeship) and her *Ausbildung* (training).
- After studying the questions carefully, try this one without a dictionary and listen to the interview without any breaks or repetitions.
- Try to get the gist of her comments so that you can draw conclusions about the five statements. Note your first thoughts in pencil, then listen a second time to get more answers or check them.
- After checking your score, you may want to listen a third time, pausing more often, to see where the answers came from.

Jetzt hören Sie ein Interview mit Petra.

Wenn die Aussage richtig ist, schreiben Sie ein **R**.
Wenn die Aussage falsch ist, schreiben Sie ein **F**.

Beispiel: Petra verdient schon sehr gut.   F

    a Einige Leute kommen direkt zu Petra, wenn sie etwas kaufen wollen.

    b Petra möchte später einmal ihren eigenen Laden haben.

    c Man lernt sehr viel, wenn man in einem Kaufhaus arbeitet.

    d Petra hat schon ihre erste Prüfung gehabt.

    e Petra wird nach der Ausbildung in diesem Kaufhaus bleiben und arbeiten. [5 marks]

© MEG Specimen Papers 1997/8

(Solution: page 108)

13 Careers and employment

- You have to answer this question in German. Look at the example. You can see that your answer need only be short, not a full sentence. Examiners often give an example answer to show you how to do the question, so that you don't write the wrong kind of answer. Make a point of studying any examples you are given to check on what kind of answer is expected.

Dein Freund spricht über sein Berufspraktikum. Schreib, was er sagt, für a, b und c.

Beispiel: bei wem   *bei seinem Onkel*

    a Arbeitsplatz   **b** Aufgaben   **c** Arbeitszeiten [3 marks]

© London Examinations, a division of Edexcel Foundation 1996

(Solution: page 108)

Listening
Part 2

14 Careers and employment

◆ This next question has a series of pictures for you to put in the right order. Here the visuals will help you understand, if you think about them beforehand. Try to think of a key word for each picture, for example *Computer* and *Brief*, and listen out for those words.

◆ By now your exam technique and understanding should be improving nicely. Try to be stricter with yourself as the exam date approaches, and tackle some of the questions as if it was an exam.

Michaels Arbeitstag – ordne die Bilder. Hör zu. Es gibt sieben Sätze.
Schreib 1–7 und die passenden Buchstaben. [5 marks]

Beispiel: 3. A 7. C

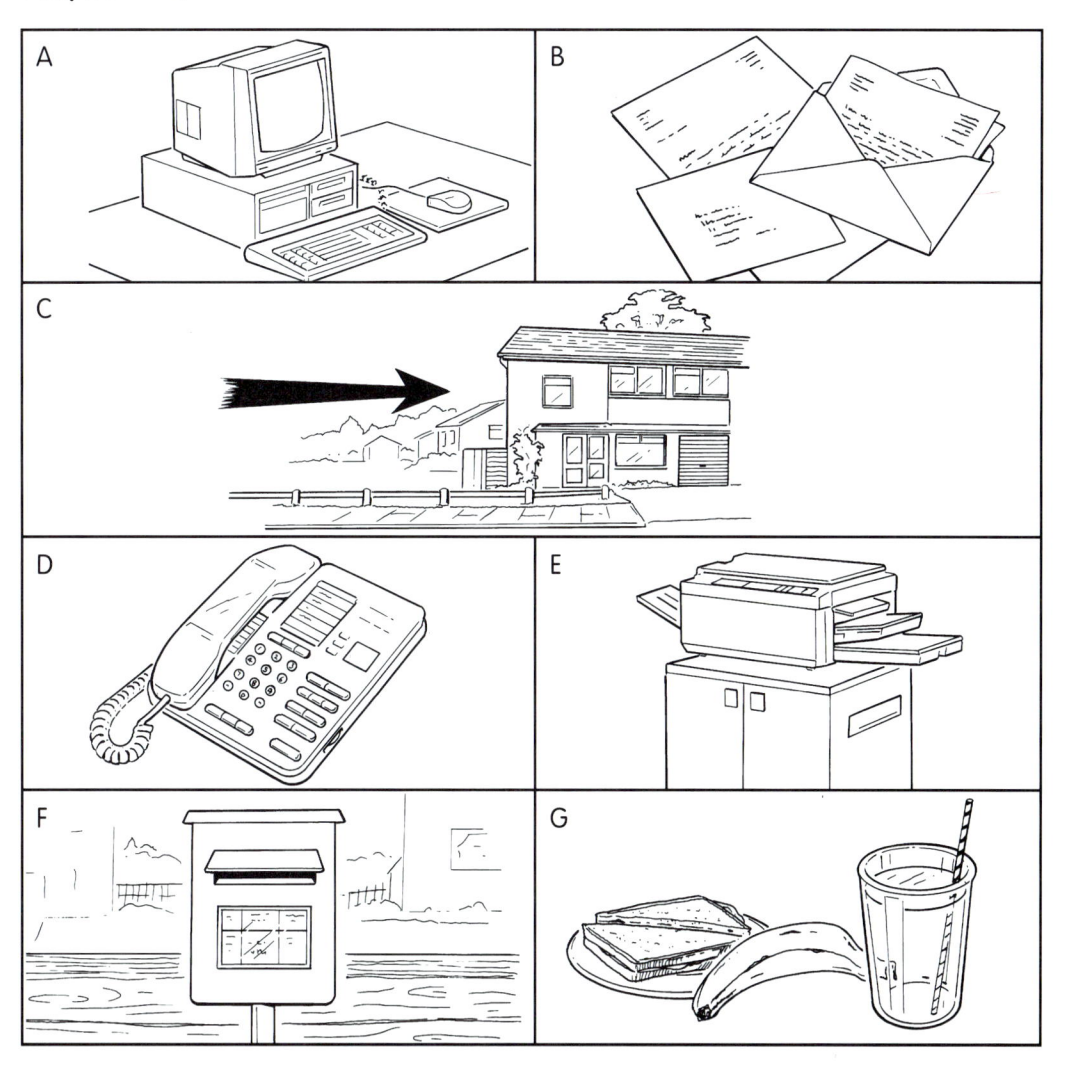

(Solution: page 108) © Northern Examinations and Assessment Board 1996

Listening
Part 2

E The international world

15 Tourism

> ◘ Once again, you will gain marks if you read the questions carefully before listening to the recording. You could also perhaps choose one word to check in the dictionary, for example *Sehenswürdigkeiten*.

Du bist in Deutschland. Du planst einen Ausflug mit Freunden. Schreib, ob der Satz richtig (**R**) oder falsch (**F**) ist.

- **a** Die Freunde fahren im Sommer.
- **b** Sie bleiben in der Jugendherberge.
- **c** Es ist teuer in der Jugendherberge.
- **d** Sie wollen sich die Sehenswürdigkeiten ansehen.
- **e** Sie hat Karten für einen Film.
- **f** Das Hard Rock Café hat Susi gefallen. [6 marks]

© Welsh Joint Education Committee 1995

(Solution: page 108)

16 Accommodation

> ◘ If you have followed the advice given earlier, you should know your German numbers very well by now. If that is the case, you will be able to score high marks on a question such as this one. Whenever you have a recording of an answering machine to listen to, there is a very good chance it will contain telephone numbers and times – make sure you are well-prepared!
>
> ◘ Study the question very carefully and use the visuals to help you. If you think of German words to match the pictures, you will be ready to recognise them.
>
> ◘ The page looks very full and confusing at first, but remember that examiners usually set the questions in the same order as the recording, so you can work through it logically from the top.

Listening Part 2

Was kann man in Boppard machen? Du hörst die telefonische Touristen-Info.
Schreib die Buchstaben von den Informationen oder Bildern, die zum Text passen. [12 marks]

1 (ship)	A nach Rüdesheim	D morgen 9.00 Uhr
	B nach Koblenz	E morgen 9.30 Uhr
	C morgen 8.30 Uhr	
2 (train)	A nach Rüdesheim	
	B nach Boppard	
	C nach Buchholz	
3 Rheinexpreß	A Sonntag bis Samstag	D zwischen 10.00 u. 6.00 Uhr
	B Montags	E zwischen 10.30 u. 18.00 Uhr
	C Freitags	F zwischen 10.20 u. 18.00 Uhr
4 (people)	A Dienstag	D vormittags
	B Donnerstag	E nachmittags
	C Freitag	F abends
5 (chairlift)	A (forest/fields)	D (cup of coffee)
	B (lake)	E (cheese)
	C (mountains)	F (chicken leg)
6 (telephone)		A 0 67 42 38 88
		B 0 67 44 88 88
		C 0 67 42 83 88

© SEG Specimen Papers 1997

(Solution: page 108)

17 Accommodation

> ◊ This question is a useful model for a rôleplay. When you have done the exercise and checked your score, play the recording through a few times. Try to memorise it until you can speak along with it, without looking at the tapescript.

Richtig oder falsch? Schreib **R** (richtig) oder **F** (falsch) für a–d.

Beispiel: Das Hotel heißt Rheinblick. *R*

  a Die Reservierung ist auf den Namen Gisbert.
  b Er hat für drei Nächte reserviert.
  c Das Zimmer ist im fünften Stock.
  d Man kann den Fluß vom Fenster sehen. [4 marks]

(Solution: page 108)

Listening: Part 3

In Part 3, you can learn how to do everything you need to earn a grade A*:

- **Everything in Part 2** (see page 29).
- **Understand gist and identify main points and details** in a variety of types of authentic spoken German.
- **Recognise points of view, attitudes and emotions.**
- **Draw conclusions.**

A Everyday activities

1 School

- This first question about school life offers a good range of opinions from two teenagers.
- Read the questions carefully, so that you have a focus for your listening when you start to play the recording.
- The most useful technique to adopt here is that of writing key words in German, while listening. The recording is quite long though, so you may not be able to remember all the German vocabulary you need to formulate your answer. Of course, you may answer in your own German words, if you can remember the details but not the actual words used.
- You need not write in sentences and the most important aspect is communicating the correct information, not the accuracy of your spelling or grammar.
- When you have completed the questions and checked your score, why not read the tapescript and write down some useful sentences you could use in your speaking test to express opinions about your school? By changing the lessons and some of the describing words you could create sentences of your own.

Alexandra und Nicola sprechen über die Schule. Was sagen sie (auf deutsch) von:

- **a** den Lehrern im allgemeinen
- **b** dem Religionslehrer
- **c** der Disziplin
- **d** der Klasse
- **e** der Englischstunde
- **f** der englischen Grammatik [6 marks]

(Solution: page 108)

Listening
Part 3

2 Health and fitness

- In this exercise you will hear simple past verbs like *wollte*, *waren*, *fühlten*, which are used for description in the past.

- Many verbs are in the perfect tense and you will hear, for example *habe ... gekauft*, with the past participle at the end of the sentence, as you would expect. There are also more complicated examples of word order, but the key to the meaning of the verb is usually the past participle beginning with *ge-*, or which has *ge-* somewhere near the beginning. Examples such as *Geschmeckt hat's nicht* and *als du angefangen hast* will also occur.

- Give only a brief answer; sometimes one word will do.

Richard, Karin und Günter erzählen, wie sie zu rauchen angefangen haben. Hör gut zu, und beantworte dann die folgenden Fragen oder füll die Lücken aus. Schreib nur ein paar Wörter.

    a Richard war ... Jahre alt, als er zu rauchen angefangen hat.
    b Was wollten Richard und seine Freunde machen?
    c Wie hat Richard seine erste Zigarette geschmeckt?
    d Wie fühlten Richard und seine Freunde sich, als sie rauchten?
    e Wer hat Karin ihre erste Zigarette gegeben?
    f Wie alt war Karin, als sie ihre erste Zigarette geraucht hat?
    g Wie hat Karin sich gefühlt?
    h Von wem hat Günter seine erste Zigarette gehabt?
    i Wie alt war Günter, als er seine erste Zigarette geraucht hat?
    j Seit Günter nicht mehr raucht, fühlt er sich ...
    k Was kann Günter jetzt besser machen?
    l ... und?
    m ... und?

[13 marks]

© SEG Specimen Papers 1997

(Solution: page 108)

3 Health and fitness

- The marks will tell you how much information to give.

Beantworte die Fragen auf deutsch.

    a Warum probiert Jan keine Drogen? [2]
    b Warum nehmen manche seiner Klassenkameraden Drogen? [3]
    c Was denkt Jan über seine Klassenkameraden, die Drogen nehmen? [1]   [6 marks]

© London Examinations, a division of Edexcel Foundation 1996

(Solution: page 108)

Listening Part 3

4 Food

> ◆ The instructions in this example are very helpful, so take time to read them before you read the questions. Allow yourself three minutes to study the questions and to look up any key words in the dictionary. Don't go over your time because it is limited in the exam.
>
> ◆ You will only need one or two words to answer each question, so try to work out from each question what words are likely. For example, in **a** you are looking for an adjective to complete their opinion. It could be *gut, lecker, frisch, weich, ohne Geschmack, schrecklich, knusprig* and so on. In **c**, you are looking for a number; in **d**, something to eat for breakfast. Once again, the technique of writing down key German words as you listen will also help you to write your answers.

Einige deutsche Schüler sprechen über das Essen in Deutschland und England.

Wichtig: Denk nicht darüber nach, was du denkst, sondern darüber, was die drei jungen Deutschen meinen!

Schreib diese Sätze aus, oder beantworte die Fragen (schreib nur ein paar Wörter).

a Heinz und Christian finden englisches Brot …

b In England hat Christian kein … gesehen.

c Christian meint, in Deutschland gibt es … Sorten von Brot.

d Heinz hätte gern zum Frühstück … gegessen.

e Steffi findet … gesünder in England als in Deutschland.

f Wer hat bei der englischen Familie viel gegessen?

g Steffi meint: In Deutschland ißt man … Fleisch.

h Steffis Gastmutter sagt: Gemüse ist gesund, aber nur wenn …

i Wie lange war Christian bei der englischen Familie?

j In Christians englischer Familie sind alle …

k Warum sind Pommes nicht gesund, meint Steffi?

l Zu Hause ißt Christian immer viel Fleisch, denn sein Onkel …

m Die englische Familie, bei der Steffi war, hat viele Pommes gegessen, damit die … Kartoffeln essen.

[13 marks]

(Solution: page 109)

B Personal and social life

5 Self, family and friends

> ◆ The reason the robber gives for being in the shop is for an activity you would normally expect to hear about in a different location. This tests one of the skills mentioned at the beginning of Part 2, namely: 'understanding familiar language in unfamiliar contexts'.
>
> ◆ Remember, if you hear a key word of which you do not know the meaning, write it down in pencil at the side and look it up at the end if you have time.

You hear a report of a robbery on the radio while driving with your parents in Germany. Answer the questions in English.

a What reason did the robber give the manageress for coming into the shop? [1]

b How was he disguised? [2] [3 marks]

© London Examinations, a division of Edexcel Foundation 1996

(Solution: page 109)

6 Self, family and friends

> ◆ The second question tests your understanding of descriptions of character and personality and expressing feelings about others.
>
> ◆ The statements you have to make decisions about must be studied carefully before listening to the recording.
>
> ◆ At this level you will not hear the same vocabulary being used in the recording as is written in the statements. You must listen for words which mean the same, or express the same idea. To prepare for this, try to think of other ways you know of saying the four statements. Don't get worried if nothing comes to mind, because you often recognise meanings in German, even if you can't remember how to produce those words yourself. This is known as 'passive vocabulary' – it is very useful both in listening and reading!

Hör das Gespräch an und schreib den richtigen Namen, Peter oder Anna, für a–d.

a Versteht sich gut mit der Mutter.
b Muß zu Hause viel tun.
c Versteht sich gut mit dem Vater.
d Verbringt nicht viel Zeit mit dem Vater. [4 marks]

© London Examinations, a division of Edexcel Foundation 1996

(Solution: page 109)

Listening Part 3

7 Free time, holidays and special occasions

> ○ The questions in German are very precise and you will need to read them very carefully to focus your attention on specific information in the recording.
>
> ○ You must answer in German but you do not have to write full sentences and your answers will not be marked for the accuracy of the language.
>
> ○ The marks will tell you how many details to give.
>
> ○ Before you start the exercise, study the short list of phrases below. These phrases are used to express opinions in the recording.
>
> ○ Use your dictionary to practise looking words up quickly. Remember, you must look up verbs in the infinitive form, e.g. *meinen,* but also include the prefix of separable verbs, e.g. *ich gebe zu* (*zugeben*). Look for the prefix later in the phrase or sentence.
>
> *ich meine*   *davon bin ich nicht gerade*
> *meinetwegen*   *begeistert*
> *ich gebe zu*   *ich finde, daß …*
>
> These words will also be very useful for your speaking exam – you need to express opinions in German to achieve the highest grades.

Manfred und seine Tante Hildegard reden über Musik. Beantworten Sie die Fragen auf deutsch.

Abschnitt 1 Lesen Sie die Fragen a–d. Und jetzt hören Sie Abschnitt 1.

　a　Wann war Tante Hildegard in der Oper? [1]
　b　Wie hat Tante Hildegard die Aufführung gefunden? [1]
　c　Welche Kritik äußert Manfred an Opern? [2]
　d　Welche Kritik äußert Manfreds Tante an Popmusik? [2]　　[6 marks]

Abschnitt 2 Lesen Sie die Fragen e–h. Jetzt hören Sie Abschnitt 2.

　e　Warum findet Manfred Popmusik so gut? [3]
　f　Inwiefern haben Manfred und seine Tante die gleiche Meinung zu Popmusik? [1]
　g　Was ist für Manfreds Tante der wichtigste Unterschied zwischen Opern und Popmusik?　　i) Oper [1]
　　　　　　　　　　　　　　　　　　　　　　　　　　　　　ii) Popmusik [1]
　h　Welche Kritik äußert Manfreds Tante an der heutigen Jugend? [1]　　[7 marks]

(Solution: page 109)　　　　　© MEG Specimen Papers 1997/8

Listening
Part 3

8 Free time, holidays and special occasions

- This question also looks for opinions, particularly in the last part. You have to express your opinion about the family you hear in the recording. To do this you must listen not only to what is said, but also how they say it.

- You may need to use your dictionary to check some of the adjectives you are given to choose from.

Der englische Gast fährt bald nach Hause. Was wollen seine deutschen Gastgeber am letzten Wochenende mit ihm unternehmen?

1 a Erste Idee?   **2 a** Zweite Idee?   **3 a** Dritte Idee?

    b Warum nicht?   **b** Warum nicht?   **b** Gute Idee, aber … [6]

4 Wie findest du diese Familie? Wähle **zwei** Adjektive von dieser Liste.

    großzügig, schüchtern, unfreundlich, unternehmungslustig, hilfreich, gutgelaunt, streng   [2]

[8 marks]

© Northern Examinations and Assessment Board 1996

(Solution: page 109)

9 Personal relationships and social activities

- If you familiarise yourself with the written statements you will more easily recognise who would say what.

- Try to note down a letter in pencil after listening for the first time, then use the second time to confirm your answer and write the letter in pen.

Michael, Ralf, Barbara und Anja sprechen von ihren Eltern.

Wähl für jeden Teenager einen Buchstaben aus und schreib ihn auf. Lies zuerst die Sätze A – H.

Beispiel: Anja   H

A Meine Mutter hilft mir, Kleidung auszuwählen.
B Ich muß meiner Mutter viel helfen, weil sie für ihr Diplom studiert.
C Wenn ich spät nach Hause komme, sagen meine Eltern nichts.
D Ich gehe selten mit meinen Eltern aus.
E Mein Vater ist sehr sportlich.
F Meine Eltern sind immer ärgerlich, wenn ich nicht üben will.
G Ich muß jeden Abend zwei Stunden Hausaufgaben machen.
H Ich spiele überhaupt nicht gern Musik.

1 Michael
2 Ralf
3 Barbara
4 Anja

[4 marks]

(Solution: page 109)

Listening
Part 3

C The **world around** us

10 Home town, local environment and customs

> ◘ You now have three questions which you should work through one after the other, using the techniques you have learnt earlier in the book. Look back at the advice in Part 2 as well as that in Part 3. Then listen twice to each recording, writing your answers as you do so.
>
> ◘ When you have done the questions and checked your score, take some time to study the transcript thoroughly and choose some phrases or sentences you could adapt for your writing or speaking exam. To score well at higher exams you need to be able to express opinions and feelings about such things as where you live.

1 Hermann spricht über den Karneval in seiner Stadt.

Wenn die Aussage richtig ist, schreiben Sie ein **R**.
Wenn die Aussage falsch ist, schreiben Sie ein **F**.

Beispiel: Ingeborg kam aus Süddeutschland.   *F*

Abschnitt 1
Lesen Sie die Fragen a–e. Und jetzt hören Sie Abschnitt 1.

a Die Norddeutschen haben keine richtige Vorstellung vom Karneval.

b Hermann und Ingeborg gingen am Montag zum Karneval.

c Ingeborg wollte zuerst nur zu Hause bleiben.

d Als sie das Haus verließen, hielt Ingeborg einige Luftballons in der Hand.

e Ingeborg trug den Hut nicht, den ihr Hermann gab.   [5 marks]

Abschnitt 2
Lesen Sie die Fragen f–l. Und jetzt hören Sie Abschnitt 2.

f Die Leute liefen aus der Stadt.

g Die Leute hatten bunte Kleider an.

h Hermann und Ingeborg waren in der Fußgängerzone.

i Sie gingen zusammen in die Kirche.

j Ingeborg war erstaunt, als sie die Leute auf der Straße sah.

k Ingeborg bemerkte, daß die Leute Musik spielten.

l Hermann sah ein paar Fernsehkameras auf der Straße.   [7 marks]

© MEG Specimen Papers 1997/8

Listening
Part 3

2 Wer sagt was? Schreib entweder Anna oder Boris.

  a Hat vorher in der Stadt gewohnt.

  b Wohnt nicht weit von der Stadt.

  c Würde lieber in der Stadt wohnen.

  d Kann leicht in die Stadt und aufs Land fahren. [4 marks]

© London Examinations, a division of Edexcel Foundation 1996

3 Hör bitte den Text an. Stefan spricht über seine Freizeit. Beantworte bitte die Fragen.

  a Warum muß Stefan seine Freizeit anders planen als sein Freund? [2]

  b Wie kommt er in die Stadt? [1]

  c Wie macht sein Freund das? [1]

  d Was ist besser in der Stadt? [3]

  e Was macht Stefans Freund im Augenblick? [1]

  f Was sagt Stefan über die Situation im Winter? [2]

  g Wie ist das, wenn man selbst kein Auto hat? [2] [12 marks]

© SEG Specimen Papers 1997

(Solutions: page 109)

11 Shopping

> ◘ These questions must be answered in German and once more the key words technique will be a great help in formulating your answers.
>
> ◘ Note the number of marks after each question: [2] means that two pieces of information are expected.

1 Beantworte die Fragen auf deutsch.

  a Was denkt Lotte über Mode? [1]

  b Was trägt Lotte am liebsten? [2]

  c Woher bekommt sie ihre Kleider? [2] [5 marks]

© London Examinations, a division of Edexcel Foundation 1996

2 Apfelkuchen.
Bitte die Einkaufsliste schreiben.
Beispiel: 500 g Äpfel [5 marks]

© Northern Examinations and Assessment Board 1996

(Solutions: page 109)

Listening Part 3

3 Vatis Geburtstag.

   a Schreib den Buchstaben von dem Geschenk, das sie kaufen.

   b Schreib, warum sie dieses Geschenk wählen.

   c Schreib, warum sie die **zwei** anderen nicht kaufen.   [4 marks]

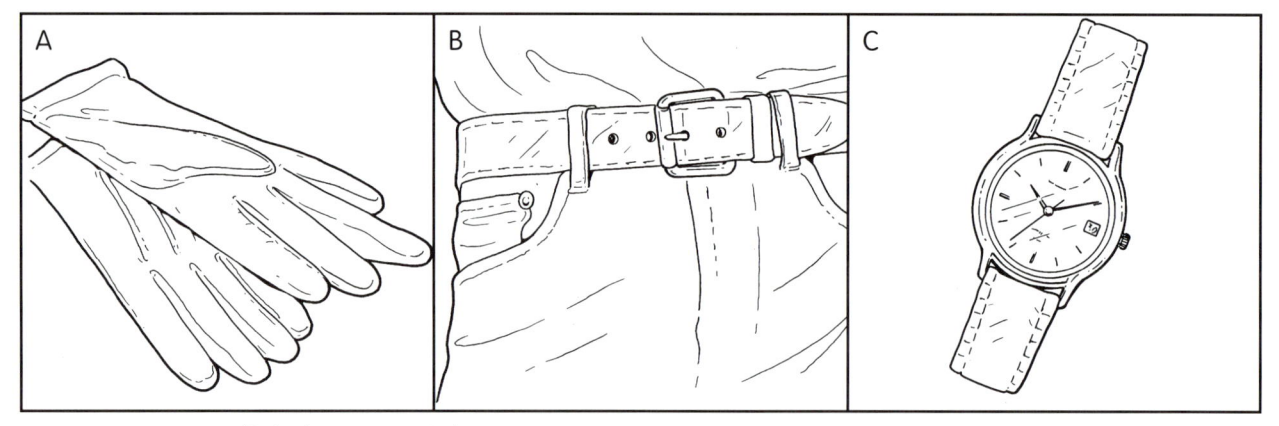

A   B   C

(Solution: page 109)

12 Getting around

> These two questions need answers in English. If, after careful listening, you cannot think of the English meaning, write down the German equivalent as exactly as you can, in pencil at the side, just as you practised earlier. You can then look the word(s) up during the dictionary time allowed and gain extra marks. You may gain enough to take you up to the next grade!

1 Frau Müller and Werner are talking about their opinions of England. Answer **in English**.

   A Travelling by car in England
   What is Frau Müller's opinion?   [1 mark]

   B Public transport in England
   What is Werner's opinion? Choose a or b and give a reason.
   a Not as good as in Germany;
   b Better than in Germany   [2 marks]

   © MEG Specimen Papers 1997/8

2 You are driving with your parents in Germany and you hear the following report about a traffic accident. Explain **in English** what has happened.

   a Give details of the casualties.

   b How did the accident happen?

   c What did the police do?   [3 marks]

   © London Examinations, a division of Edexcel Foundation 1996

(Solutions: page 110)

D The world of work

13 Careers and employment

- This section is often tested in your exam, so make sure you have revised the key vocabulary for it.

- Now you can practise answering a series of questions all in one go. Don't get depressed if you find a question difficult and, above all, don't give up or stop trying. Just draw a cross in pencil next to the question and write any key words of German you heard.

- At the end of the exam you will have time to go back to those questions with your dictionary. You must keep going: the next question could be much easier.

- In most exams, the difficulty level of the questions fluctuates, so that you often have an easier question after a hard one. Always keep going and try to stay calm and optimistic.

- Before you start, remember all the things you have learnt about preparation and stategies for listening and writing your answers. Give yourself four minutes to read all these questions and look up a few carefully chosen words if you need to. Listen to each recording twice only, as in the real exam. When you check your score you will be able to see what progress you have made.

1 Hör bitte den Text an. Beantworte dann die Fragen. Die Informationen sind über die Studienpläne eines deutschen Mädchens.

  a Bis zu welcher Klasse will sie am Gymnasium bleiben? [1]
  b Was macht sie dann? [1]
  c Wie alt ist sie dann? [1]
  d Mit wem will sie dann arbeiten? [1]
  e Wo? [1]
  f Wie lange dauert die Arbeit? [1]
  g Was kann sie schon gut sprechen? [1]
  h Was möchte sie studieren? [1]
  i Was genau möchte sie werden? [2]
  j Wie lange ist das Studium dafür? [1]
  k Wo hat sie schon einmal gearbeitet? [1]   [12 marks]

(Solution: page 110)   © SEG Specimen Papers 1997

Listening
Part 3

2 Stellenangebote im Radio.

  a Welche Stelle wird angeboten?

  b Welche Stelle wird angeboten, und welche Eigenschaft ist wichtig? [2 marks]

  © London Examinations, a division of Edexcel Foundation 1996

3 Du hörst ein Interview mit drei jungen Deutschen über das Berufspraktikum. Beantworte die Fragen!

  Monika
  a Wo hat Monika gearbeitet?
  b Wie lange war sie dort?
  c Wie lange wird sie jeden Samstag arbeiten?

  Georg
  a Wie hat er sein Berufspraktikum gefunden?
  b Wo hat er im Hotel gearbeitet?
  c Was war für ihn positiv da?

  Markus
  a Wie hat Markus sein Berufspraktikum gefunden?
  b Wann mußte er aufstehen?
  c Was würde er nie wieder machen? [9 marks]

  © Welsh Joint Education Committee 1995

4 Your penfriend's mother is talking about working in Germany. Write down notes in English for a school project.

  a What is different about the German pattern of work? [1]

  b Which routine does she prefer and why? [2]

  c Name one advantage and one disadvantage of the job. [2]

  d What does she intend to do in September? [1] [6 marks]

  © London Examinations, a division of Edexcel Foundation 1996

5 Das Leben früher und heutzutage.
Der 70jährige Jürgen vergleicht sein Leben vor vierzig Jahren mit dem Leben heutzutage. Was sagt er über:

  – Arbeit
  – Ferien
  – Geld
  – Lebensstandard
  – Familie

  a vor vierzig Jahren? [5]
  b jetzt? [5] [10 marks]

  © Northern Examinations and Assessment Board 1996

(Solutions: page 110)

14 Communication

- The telephone answering machine was welcomed by listening test examiners who often use it as a stimulus for an exam question. Very often the message will include telephone numbers, dates and times. You can earn a great number of marks in the listening exam simply by knowing your German numbers really well. You'd be surprised how many people don't and thereby lose marks. Don't be one of them!

- In this question, you choose the correct answer from pictures or from German words; some answers must be written in German.

- You can prepare yourself in the usual way by thinking of German words for the pictures and by reading the German thoroughly.

- For the last three questions, listen for key words in German and write them down in pencil.

Du hörst die Telefongespräche vom automatischen Anrufbeantworter ab. Du findest diese Mitteilung von der Firma Müller in Hamburg. Schreib die Buchstaben von den Bildern und Wörtern, die zum Text passen. [11 marks]

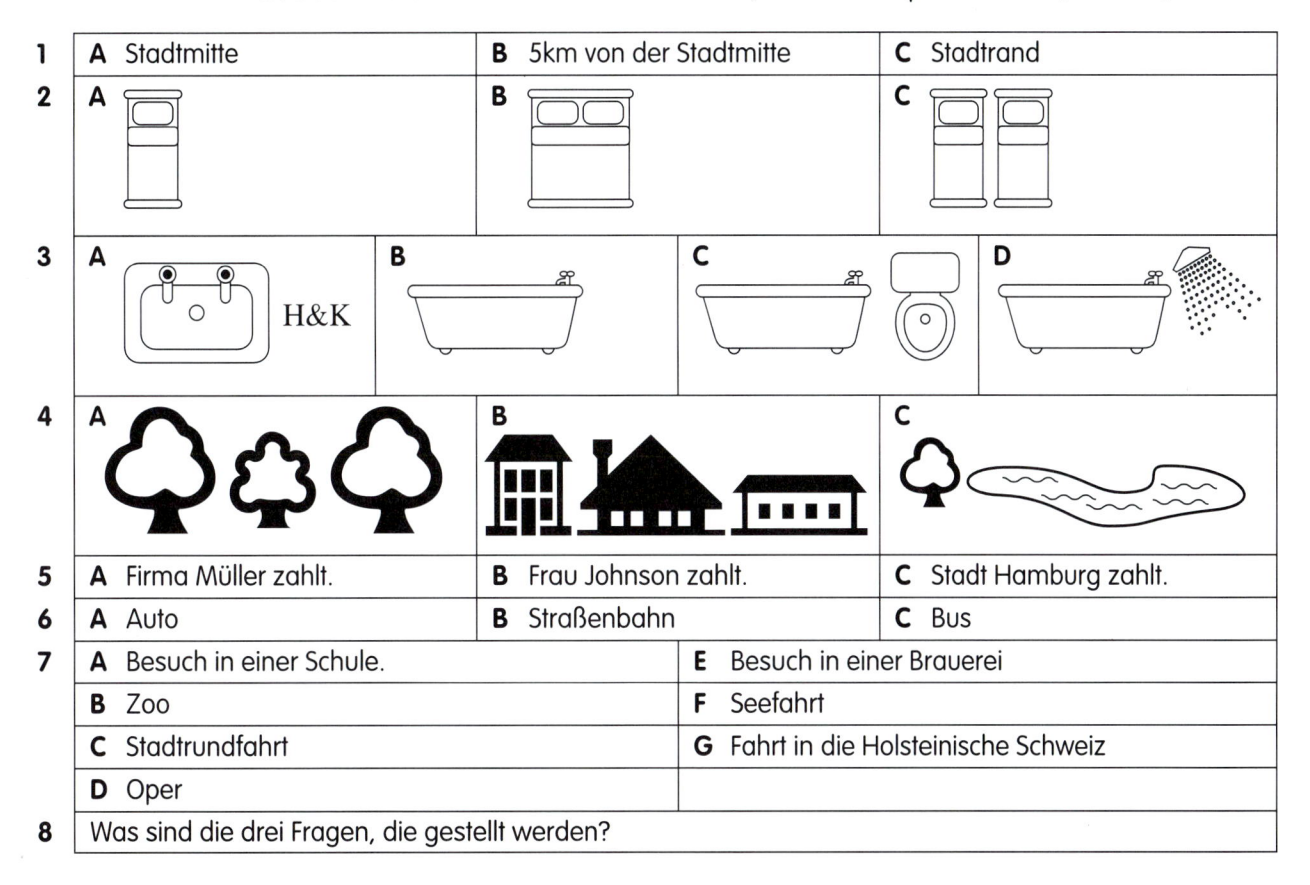

1	A Stadtmitte	B 5km von der Stadtmitte	C Stadtrand	
2	A	B	C	
3	A H&K	B	C	D
4	A	B	C	
5	A Firma Müller zahlt.	B Frau Johnson zahlt.	C Stadt Hamburg zahlt.	
6	A Auto	B Straßenbahn	C Bus	
7	A Besuch in einer Schule.		E Besuch in einer Brauerei	
	B Zoo		F Seefahrt	
	C Stadtrundfahrt		G Fahrt in die Holsteinische Schweiz	
	D Oper			
8	Was sind die drei Fragen, die gestellt werden?			

(Solution: page 110)

Listening
Part 3

E The international world

15 Tourism

- This first question has a very short recording of a radio advert, with facts that are quite easy to remember.

- Because this is a higher tier question the examiner is expecting a precise answer for Number 1 and some verbs for Number 2, not simply the nouns you will hear.

- The question reads *Was kann man dort **machen***?, which shows that these activities are required.

FERIEN

Im Radio hörst du die folgende Reklame. Beantworte die Fragen auf deutsch.

   a Wohin kann man fahren? [1]

   b Was kann man dort machen? [2]   [3 marks]

© London Examinations, a division of Edexcel Foundation 1996

(Solution: page 110)

16 Tourism

- The second question needs careful reading of the alternative answers you are to choose from in order to focus your listening. Also try to think of German words to match the four pictures in Number 3.

1 Du machst mit einer Stadtführerin eine Tour durch Köln. Welcher Satz ist richtig? Schreib A, B oder C.

   A Die Tour beginnt in der Altstadt.

   B Die Tour endet am Dom.

   C Die Tour dauert anderthalb Stunden. [1]

2 Welcher Satz ist richtig? Schreib A, B oder C.

   A Die Führerin lädt die Touristen zum Frühstück ein.

   B Die Touristen haben das Mittagessen schon bezahlt.

   C Das Mittagessen ist in einem modernen Restaurant. [1]

Listening
Part 3

3 Was machst du jetzt? Schreib A, B, C und D in der richtigen Reihenfolge. [4] [6 marks]

© London Examinations, a division of Edexcel Foundation 1996

(Solution: page 110)

17 Accommodation

- This question revises a good selection of accommodation vocabulary in the advert you have to read before you listen.

- Then you can use the recording tapescript, after checking your answers, to note some useful phrases for complaining about hotel facilities in your speaking or writing exams.

- Tanya is so cross that you will also hear a good range of negative German expressions:
  nicht   kein
  noch nicht   weder ... noch
  nie   nichts
  If you are not sure of any of these, practise looking them up in your dictionary at speed.

PARKHOTEL
Tanya war gar nicht zufrieden.
Das Hotel war nicht so gut.
Schreib die Buchstaben von drei weiteren Sätzen, die falsch sind.

Beispiel: b

 a Dieses erstklassige Hotel befindet sich in ruhiger Lage.
 b Die Zimmer sind mit Bad oder Dusche.
 c Alle Zimmer verfügen über Telefon, Radio und Farbfernseher.
 d Das Fitneßcenter bietet Hallenbad und Sauna.
 e Tischtennis und Billard sind im Preis inbegriffen.
 f Für Sonnenbäder steht eine Sonnenterrasse zur Verfügung.
 g Morgens gibt es ein Frühstücksbüffet.
 h Abends bieten wir ein viergängiges Menü.   [3 marks]

(Solution: page 110)   © Northern Examinations and Assessment Board 1996

18 The wider world

◆ This question is divided into three parts so that you don't have to remember too much information at once. You must read the questions very carefully and before you start, quickly check two or three selected words in your dictionary. Remember, you will not have much time in the exam, so choose only the key words.

◆ These true or false questions may appear easy but the examiner will make slight changes to the words, for example *ein* becomes *kein*, or will use words which mean the same or occur in the same sentence. All in all, you need to listen extremely attentively.

JUNGE LEUTE UND DIE UMWELT

Schreib **R** (richtig) oder **F** (falsch) für die folgenden Sätze.

   a Die Familie sortiert den Müll.
   b Die Familie macht nichts für die Umwelt.
   c Die Familie spart Energie.
   d Die Temperatur im Haus ist 2°.
   e Energiesparen spart auch Geld.
   f Die Familie kauft nur Ökoprodukte.
   g Ökoprodukte sind nicht billig.
   h Das größte Problem für die Umwelt in Deutschland ist der Lärm.
   i Deutschland hat zu viele Autos. [9 marks]

© Welsh Joint Education Board 1995

(Solution: page 110)

How to prepare for your speaking exam

The more you know about how your speaking exam works and how what you say is marked, the better your result will be, so look carefully at the syllabus and ask your teacher to explain it to you. This section will show you how to do well in all the tasks you will have to do in your exam. Work through it and practise along the lines suggested and you will get the best possible grade. One thing to remember is that you can get high marks in your speaking exam by using what you have learnt to write, and that you can use in your writing exam what you have learnt to say. So, you don't have to learn everything twice!

The exam

In your speaking exam, you will have two sorts of activities: two rôle-plays and a conversation. About half the marks go to each of these, so both are important. You can score the highest marks if you remember a few important points:

1 In rôle-plays, what really matters is that you communicate the messages so that a German person would understand them. Concentrate on this, keep what you say as simple as possible and don't worry if you make a few mistakes.

2 In the conversation, the examiner wants to hear just how good your German is and how much you know. This section of the book will show you how to demonstrate this to your best advantage.

It is also useful to remember that your conversation will be with your teacher: your teacher will ask the questions and will ask the same sorts of questions in the exam as s/he asks in class, and as are in this book. So listen carefully in class to the questions and practise answering them as much as possible. What you do in this book and in class is what you will do in the exam.

How to use the book and cassette

Work regularly with the book and cassette for the year before your exam.

Each topic deals with either rôle-play or conversation, or both, depending on the way it is more likely to be tested in the exam.

Model answers are provided for all questions. However, in some cases, the answers follow immediately after the question and are accompanied by explanations and advice: these are designed to help you learn best how to tackle that particular type of question. Other questions are provided so that you can test yourself, in which case you will find the suggested answers at the back in the Solutions.

The earlier topics in this section give you more help with ways to tackle the rôle-plays and conversations than the later ones, so you will probably find it helpful to work through the section in order.

You can follow the steps below with each rôle-play and conversation.

1 Work on the vocabulary for each topic in *GCSE German Vocabulary* (Heinemann) and make sure you know all the key words.

2 Look at the rôle-play or questions and prepare them along the lines suggested.

3 If you feel confident, you can then listen to the recording and pause the cassette to say your answers. Check with the Solutions and listen to the model answers. Finally, try to learn the model answers or adapt them to talk about yourself and write them down. Ask your teacher to correct your German and learn your own model answers.

4 If, when you look at a rôle-play or some questions, you need help, you can look at the model answers in the Solutions. Follow the model answers in the book as you listen to them on the cassette. Try to learn the answers. Then look again at the questions and prepare to answer them. Now play the recording and pause the cassette to say your answers. Finally, adapt answers to talk about yourself. Write them and ask your teacher to correct your German. Learn your own model answers.

How to learn the model answers

The more model answers you learn by heart, the better you will do in your exam. Here is a system which will help you to learn:

1 Listen to the model answers, pause the recording and repeat immediately after each sentence. If a sentence is too long for you to do this, pause in the middle and repeat. Another good technique with long sentences is to break them up into easy sections and to repeat them in short sections, starting with the last section. Take a sentence like this: *Ich bin letztes Jahr mit der Schule nach Iserlohn in Deutschland gefahren.*
First, repeat:
   ... in Deutschland gefahren.
When you feel confident with that, repeat:
   ... nach Iserlohn in Deutschland gefahren.
Then practise saying:
   ... mit der Schule nach Iserlohn in Deutschland gefahren.
Then add:
   ... letztes Jahr mit der Schule nach Iserlohn in Deutschland gefahren.
Finally, repeat the whole sentence:
   Ich bin letztes Jahr mit der Schule nach Iserlohn in Deutschland gefahren.

2 When you find it easy to repeat **after** the model answers, practise repeating them **with** the recording. Try to say them at the same speed and with the same accent as the German people on the recording. This will help you to speak just like a German person, which will greatly impress the examiners.

3 Finally, you can practise saying the rôle-plays/conversations **without** the help of the recording. An excellent way to do this is to work with a friend. Take turns to be the teacher and give the other the chance to answer the questions or play their part in the rôle-plays.

You can sum up these three steps as: speak **after** the cassette, speak **with** the cassette and speak **without** the cassette.

Revision

You will learn best if you revise regularly. A good way of doing this is to work quickly through everything you have done so far, before you start on a new section in the book. This won't take you very long but it will make you feel much more confident.

On the day before your speaking exam and on the day of the exam before you go in, spend as much time as you can listening, on the cassette, to the model rôle-plays and conversations. Practise repeating after and with the recording.

Don't be put off by how much there seems to be for you to learn. There is much less than there appears to be: much of it is German which you already know and what this book does is to show you how to use it to gain a high grade in your speaking exam.

So, good luck and good speaking!

What the examiners are looking for in the speaking exam

Foundation Tier

You should be able to:

1 Refer to past, present and future events in rôle-plays and conversations.

2 Express personal opinions.

3 Show the ability to deal with some unpredictable elements.

4 Convey messages clearly even if you make some mistakes.

5 Speak with a German pronunciation and intonation which are generally accurate.

Higher Tier

In addition to the above, you should be able to:

1 Take the initiative in rôle-plays and conversations.

2 Narrate something that happened.

3 Express and justify ideas and points of view.

4 Produce longer sequences of speech, using a variety of vocabulary and structures.

5 Speak confidently, with good pronunciation and intonation.

As you work through this book, you will learn to meet all these requirements.

Speaking
Area A

A Everyday activities

1 School

Conversation

- In the speaking test, school is often talked about in the conversation. In this book you can learn how to understand and answer the sorts of questions most commonly asked.

- Begin by reading the questions in the two tiers you are preparing for, covering up the model answers on the right. Make sure that you understand the questions and use a dictionary if you need to.

- Listen to the recording next, concentrating on the questions. Make sure that you will recognise and easily understand them if you hear them in your exam – listen as many times as you like!

- When you feel confident about the questions, prepare your answers to them. You can use the model answers to help you, changing any of the underlined words to make them **your** answers.

- Then play the recording again. Pause after each question and answer it before listening to the recorded answer. Do this a few times and repeat any of the recorded answers you need to learn.

- Finally, try to practise with a partner, taking turns to ask and answer the questions.

Speaking
Area A

A Foundation

	Questions	Model answers
1	Wie kommst du zur Schule?	Normalerweise <u>fahre ich mit dem Bus</u>.^a Aber im Sommer <u>fahre ich mit dem Fahrrad</u>.
2	Wann beginnt die erste Stunde?	Die erste Stunde beginnt um <u>neun Uhr zehn</u>. Die Schule ist um <u>halb vier</u> aus.^b
3	Was ist dein Lieblingsfach?	Ich habe zwei Lieblingsfächer – <u>Englisch</u>, weil es ganz <u>einfach</u> ist, und <u>Mathe</u>, weil es sehr <u>nützlich</u> ist. Aber <u>Geschichte</u> habe ich nicht gern. Ich war immer schwach in <u>Geschichte</u>.^c
4	Wieviel Hausaufgaben hast du?	Meiner Meinung nach haben wir zu viel Hausaufgaben. Ich mache <u>zwei</u> Stunden pro Tag. Das ist viel, nicht wahr? ^d
5	Wo machst du deine Hausaufgaben?	Ich mache meine Hausaufgaben gewöhnlich <u>in meinem Schlafzimmer</u>. Aber gestern abend habe ich <u>im Garten</u> gearbeitet, weil das Wetter so <u>schön</u> war.^e
6	Was für Arbeitsgemeinschaften gibt es in deiner Schule?	Es gibt viele Arbeitsgemeinschaften in meiner Schule. Heute zum Beispiel gehe ich nach der Schule <u>zum Jazzklub</u>.^f

a It is very good to say what you usually (*normalerweise*) do and what you do in summer (*im Sommer*). Don't forget that if you start your German sentence with an expression of time, you must invert the verb, as you see above (*fahre ich*).

b You will impress the examiners by going further than you have to. Here you can also say when school ends.

c You really must prepare something like this about the subjects you like or dislike in school. You may be able to use it in both your speaking and writing exams.

d This is excellent because it goes beyond the minimum. It answers the question, expresses an opinion and, with *nicht wahr*, asks the examiner's opinion.

e Another excellent reply, taking the opportunity to talk about the past and say what you did yesterday evening (*gestern abend*). If you can add a clause with *weil* (because) and the verb at the end, it's even more impressive!

f Here the *Heute zum Beispiel* introduces a reference to the future: this will earn high marks. You must prepare things you can say about the past and the future, and make sure you use some of them in every conversation.

Speaking
Area A

B Foundation/Higher

	Questions	Model answers
1	Um wieviel Uhr verläßt du das Haus, um zur Schule zu gehen?	Normalerweise verlasse ich das Haus um <u>acht Uhr</u>. Aber heute bin ich um <u>zwanzig vor neun</u> weggegangen.^a
2	Bist du gern in der Schule?	Ja, ich finde meine Schule <u>gut</u>, weil die Lehrer meistens <u>sympathisch</u> sind.^b
3	Was machst du in der Mittagspause?	Ich <u>treffe mich gewöhnlich mit meinen Freunden</u>. Aber gestern habe ich für meine Prüfungen gearbeitet. Morgen <u>spiele ich Tennis</u>.^c
4	Was machst du gern, wenn du nicht in der Schule bist?	<u>Ich höre sehr gern Musik</u>. Letztes Wochenende zum Beispiel war ich in einem Konzert und, heute abend gehe ich <u>zur Disko</u>. <u>Popmusik</u> ist <u>klasse</u>.^d
5	Seit wann lernst du Deutsch?	Seit fast <u>fünf</u> Jahren. Deutsch war immer mein Lieblingsfach. Wenn ich gute Noten kriege, mache ich nächstes Jahr Deutsch.^e
6	Was möchtest du im nächsten Schuljahr machen?	Wenn ich gute Noten in meinem Examen bekomme, gehe ich in die Oberstufe. Ich werde wahrscheinlich <u>Deutsch, Englisch und Ökonomie</u> machen.^f

a An excellent answer, using *normalerweise* and a reference to the present with *heute* and a reference to the past.

b A good opinion, introduced effectively by *ich finde*, justified with *weil* and the verb sent to the correct position at the end.

c A really good answer! It uses *gewöhnlich* and a reference to the present, *gestern* with a reference to the past and *morgen* with a reference to the future.

d This answer has everything the examiners are looking for. It begins with a reference to the present, including an opinion. Then *letztes Wochenende* *zum Beispiel* introduces a reference to the past and *heute abend* introduces a reference to the future. It finishes with another opinion.

e This answer is good because it refers to past and future. It also shows initiative by saying more about German than was asked for. Whenever you can, go further than the question asks for: take over the conversation and use it to show off for the examiner some of the good things you have learnt to say.

f This contains excellent references to the future and again goes beyond a minimum answer.

Speaking
Area A

C Higher

Questions

1 Hier in der Schule müßt ihr eine Schuluniform tragen. Wie findest du das?

2 Was hältst du von deiner Schule?

3 Was möchtest du nach der Schule werden?

4 Gibt es Fächer, die du nicht gern machst?

5 Hast du andere Fremdsprachen außer Deutsch gelernt?

Model answers

Meiner Meinung nach ist die Schuluniform keine gute Idee.[a] Wenn ich die Schule verlasse, werde ich nie wieder eine Uniform anziehen.[b] Uniformen sind dumm, und unsere ist ganz einfach häßlich.[c]

Ja, im allgemeinen ist sie eine gute Schule. Ich habe besonders gern Deutsch und Englisch gelernt. Vor zwei Jahren mochte ich alle Fächer, aber jetzt finde ich Geschichte besonders langweilig.[d]

Wenn ich in zwei Jahren gute Noten kriege, gehe ich auf die Uni, weil ich Lehrer(-in) werden möchte.[e]

Ja, natürlich. Ich hasse Geschichte, weil ich immer schlechte Noten bekomme. Naturwissenschaften mache ich auch nicht gern, weil ich das schwierig und langweilig finde.[f]

Nein, aber ich möchte sehr gern Italienisch lernen.[g] Man sagt, daß es eine sehr schöne Sprache ist[h], und wenn ich Italienisch sprechen könnte, würde ich ohne Schwierigkeiten nach Italien fahren können. Und ich schwärme für Italien.[i]

a *Meiner Meinung nach* (in my opinion) signals clearly that you are expressing an opinion.

b A good link to a future verb followed immediately by another opinion in the present tense.

c The last two points plus this *ganz einfach* (quite simply) make this an excellent response.

d Some good references to the past, worth learning by heart and a good reference to the present introduced by *aber*.

e Excellent references to the future and well worth learning by heart to use in your speaking and writing tests.

f Two very good opinions both justified by a *weil*-clause, each with the verb in the correct position.

g An excellent use of the *Nein, aber...* technique. Always avoid a one word answer and use an opportunity like this to use something you have learnt to say well.

h *Man sagt, daß ...* is a very good expression to learn to introduce an idea or opinion, which doesn't need to be your own.

i If you have no special interest in foreign languages, you could say:
Nein, ich habe nur Deutsch gelernt, weil ich kein Interesse an Fremdsprachen habe. Wenn ich gute Noten kriege, mache ich Naturwissenschaften und Mathe nächstes Jahr. Another possible answer would be: *Ja, ich habe auch Französisch/Spanisch gelernt. Ich lerne es seit fast drei Jahren. Es ist ziemlich einfach und macht Spaß. Wenn ich gute Noten kriege, mache ich nächstes Jahr Deutsch, Französisch/Spanisch und Englisch.*

Speaking
Area A

2 Home life

Rôle-play

A Foundation

> ◆ Look at this rôle-play and use the instructions and the visuals to help you prepare. You only need to communicate the key messages, so keep what you say simple. Give yourself two minutes to prepare and look up in a dictionary any words you need.

ZU HAUSE

You have just arrived at a friend's house in Germany after a hot and tiring journey. Your teacher will play the part of your friend and will speak first.

Rôle-play

1 You ask where your room is.

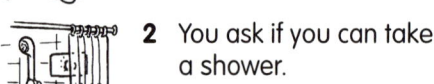

2 You ask if you can take a shower.

3 You need a towel.

4 You thank your friend.

Model answers

Lehrer(in): Wir sind bei deinem Freund/deiner Freundin in Deutschland. Ich bin dein(e) Freund(in). Ich spreche zuerst:

Also, willkommen.

Du: Danke. Wo ist mein Schlafzimmer, bitte?[a]
Lehrer(in): Hier, gegenüber vom Badezimmer.

Du: Darf ich duschen, bitte?[b]
Lehrer(in): Ja, sicher. Brauchst du etwas?

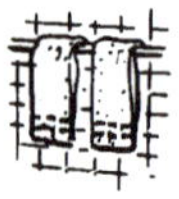

Du: Ja, ich habe kein Badetuch.[c]
Lehrer(in): Kein Problem. Du findest Handtücher und Badetücher auf deinem Bett.

Du: Danke schön.[d]

Key words and phrases

Wo ist? (Where is?);
bitte (please);
Darf ich ...? (Can I ...?);
Ich habe kein (I have no ...);
danke schön (thank you very much).

[a] Remember to say please and thank you where appropriate (*bitte* and *danke*).

[b] *Darf ich* is a very useful phrase which you should learn; you say it whenever you ask permission to do something. Remember to send the other verb to the end of the sentence, e.g *Darf ich eine CD **hören**?*

[c] You could also say here *Ich habe mein Badetuch vergessen*. Both will score full marks, so say whichever you feel most confident with.

[d] *Danke schön* is the appropriate way to say thank you to your friend here.

Speaking
Area A

B Foundation/Higher

> ◆ You have two minutes in which to prepare this rôle-play. Use both the English and the German instructions. Some exam boards use visuals to guide you through these rôle-plays, others use simple German words or short sentences.
>
> ◆ After two minutes, listen to the recording. Pause after each line said by the examiner and try to play your part before hearing it. Then check with the solution. Make sure that you can get all your responses right. Finally, work on the recording of the full rôle-play and learn your part by heart.

IN EINER DEUTSCHEN FAMILIE

You and your penfriend are going to a party this evening. You want to know what time the evening meal will be. You want to wash your hair before the meal. Answer your penfriend's question. Ask what time you will be back home after the party.

1 Frag, wann ihr eßt.

2 Sag, was du machen willst.

3 (!) Beantworte die Frage von deinem Partner/deiner Partnerin.

4 Frag, wann ihr zurückkommt.

> **1** The keyword *Frag* tells you that you have to ask a question, and here you are given a question word *wann*, which you could use.
>
> **2** The word *Sag* means that you have to say something; the English instructions make it clear.
>
> **3** The Foundation/Higher rôle-play must always have an unpredictable element in it. The exam boards tend to use a symbol such as **(!)** to warn you to be ready to respond appropriately to a question you were not able to prepare in advance. You need to listen very carefully to what your teacher says at this point.
>
> **4** Once again you have to ask when, following the English instructions.

(Solution: page 123)

Speaking
Area A

Conversation

◆ Home life is a common topic for conversation in your exam, so be prepared for it. Below are examples of the sorts of questions you will be asked. Study them and make sure you will understand them if you hear them in the exam. Many people do badly simply because they don't understand the question. Make sure this doesn't happen to you!

◆ Practise answering the questions with the book and cassette. It also helps to work with a partner if you can, taking turns to ask and answer the questions until you are both word perfect (see page 56 *How to learn the model answers*).

A Foundation

◆ Practise answering the questions on the left while covering the answers on the right. Then check the model answers, adapting any underlined words to make them your own answers.

◆ Keep your answers simple but don't be afraid to take the initiative: you could, for example, ask a question yourself.

	Questions	**Model answers**
1	Wo wohnst du?	Ich wohne <u>zehn</u> Minuten <u>zu Fuß</u> von der Schule.[a]
2	Beschreib dein Haus, bitte.	Mein Haus ist <u>ziemlich klein</u>.[b] Es gibt <u>drei</u> Schlafzimmer. Wir haben <u>eine Garage</u> und <u>einen Garten</u>.[c]
3	Was machst du zu Hause, um zu helfen?	Ich <u>decke den Tisch</u>. Gestern habe ich <u>gespült</u>.[d] Nächstes Wochenende <u>arbeite ich mit meinem Vater im Garten</u>.[e]
4	Was machst du nicht gern zu Hause?	Ich <u>spüle</u> nicht gern. Und ich hasse es, <u>den Müll rauszutragen</u>.[f] Und Sie?
5	Um wieviel Uhr gibt es bei dir Frühstück?	Normalerweise frühstücken wir gegen <u>sieben</u> Uhr. Aber am Wochenende etwas später, gegen <u>neun</u> Uhr.[g]

[a] You can vary this reply in many ways, for example *Ich wohne fünf/zwanzig/vierzig Minuten mit dem Rad/Bus/Auto von der Schule.*

[b] Using *ziemlich* is good. You could also say *Mein Haus ist ziemlich groß*.

[c] This is a very good answer because it gives several pieces of information and uses a variety of language: *Mein Haus ist ... Es gibt ...Wir haben ...* Always aim to give two or three pieces of information.

[d] Good marks here for referring to the past with *Gestern habe ich ...*

[e] More marks for referring to the future with *Nächstes Wochenende ...*

[f] This scores well by having a second example with a different verb.

[g] Another excellent answer, using *Aber ...* to bring in a second piece of information.

Speaking
Area A

B Foundation/Higher

- Again, practise answering the questions on the left first while covering the answers on the right. Then adapt the answers to your own.

- Don't forget that you are taking part in a conversation. Don't always wait for your teacher to ask questions and don't be afraid to take the conversation off in directions you want to talk about.

- You must, however, stay within the topic your teacher has chosen, because you cannot get marks for irrelevant material. This is a way to show off to the examiner some of the excellent German you have learned.

	Questions	Model answers
1	Kannst du deine Anschrift buchstabieren, bitte?	Ja, die Straße heißt <u>York Road</u>. Das schreibt man <u>Y-O-R-K</u>.
2	Wo genau liegt dein Haus?	<u>Nicht</u> weit von <u>der Schule</u>.[a] Es gibt <u>einen Supermarkt</u> in der Nähe. Das ist sehr <u>praktisch</u>, und ich mag diesen Stadtteil.[b]
3	Seit wann wohnst du dort?	Seit <u>drei</u> Jahren. Vorher wohnte ich <u>im Norden</u> und besuchte eine andere Schule.[c] Ich wohne lieber hier, weil es <u>interessanter</u> ist.[d]
4	Beschreib dein Schlafzimmer, bitte.	Ich teile mein Zimmer mit <u>meinem Bruder</u>.[e] Das Zimmer ist <u>ziemlich groß</u> und hat <u>zwei Betten, einen Kleiderschrank und einen Schreibtisch</u>.[f]
5	Wer macht normalerweise die Hausarbeit bei dir?	Meine Eltern machen fast alles, aber ich helfe am Abend. Ich <u>spüle nach dem Abendessen ab</u>. Am Wochenende <u>habe ich das Mittagessen vorbereitet. Mein Bruder</u> macht nichts, er ist sehr faul![g]

a There are numerous ways to answer this: *Sehr weit von der Schule...; Nicht weit von der Stadt in einem Dorf...; Nicht weit von der Stadtmitte...;* to mention only a few.

b Credit again for extra information and an opinion.

c A good reference to the past – seize every opportunity you come across!

d Another opinion with a good justification using *weil* with the verb in the correct position.

e Another opportunity for extra information. You may say *mit meiner Schwester* or even *Ich habe mein eigenes Zimmer* (I have my own room.)

f Always give two or three items at least, but resist the temptation to gabble pre-learned material like a parrot who doesn't understand it all!

g An excellent answer giving additional information, including a past tense, and with a touch of humour.

Speaking
Area A

C Higher

- Remember that you must refer to past, present and future, so take advantage of every chance to do this. You must also express and justify some opinions. Do both of these well if you want the highest grades.

- Try to show you can develop the conversation, using, for example:
  Ja, aber …/und …
  Zum Beispiel …

- When you are confident that you can understand all the questions, look at the suggested answers that follow.

- When you have read and understood these, listen to the recording and repeat the answers.

- Adapt the answers to say what you want to say by replacing the underlined words and write down your own version. Ask your teacher or German assistant to correct them for you. Then write a perfect copy of your answers and learn them.

- You can then play the recording again, pause after each question and say your answers.

- The same things you have learnt and practised for your speaking exam will be useful for your writing exam too, especially if you use this technique.

1 Wohnst du gern in deinem Haus?
2 Beschreib dein ideales Haus.
3 Was sind die Unterschiede zwischen deutschen und englischen Häusern?
4 Wenn es möglich wäre, möchtest du hier oder in Deutschland leben?

Speaking
Area A

Model answers

1 Ja, es ist <u>ziemlich schön</u>, aber ich möchte in einem <u>größeren Haus</u> wohnen.^a Letztes Jahr hatten wir ein schönes Ferienhaus <u>an der Küste</u>.^b Es war <u>groß und bequem</u>. Und <u>das Meer</u> war fantastisch. <u>An der Küste</u> wohnen ist viel <u>interessanter</u>, nicht wahr?^c

2 So, mein ideales Haus wäre <u>an der Küste</u>. Es wäre sehr <u>groß</u>, mit <u>zehn</u> Schlafzimmern. Ich hätte einen riesengroßen^d Garten und eine Garage für <u>fünf</u> Autos. Ich habe dieses Haus schon gesehen, als ich im Urlaub war. Es war wunderschön!

3 Also, ich war noch nie in Deutschland, aber^e ich habe Fotos von deutschen Häusern im Deutschlehrbuch gesehen. Man sagt^f, daß fast alle Häuser einen Keller haben. Hier in England ist es nicht so. Es scheint auch^g, daß viele Deutsche in Wohnungen wohnen. Ich möchte sehr gerne nach Deutschland fahren, um die schönen deutschen Häuser zu sehen.^h

4 Das ist eine schwere Frage! Da ich noch nie in Deutschland war, weiß ich es nicht. <u>Dieses Jahr</u> fahre ich <u>in den Sommerferien</u> nach Deutschland.ⁱ Nach meinem Aufenthalt werde ich diese Frage besser beantworten können. Aber ich wohne sehr gern hier, <u>weil ich viele Freunde habe</u>, und^j <u>die Stadt nicht zu langweilig ist</u>.

a *Ich möchte …* (I'd like to …), with the second verb at the end of the sentence, is a very useful phrase to use both in speaking and writing.

b A good opportunity again to bring in a past tense, which is well justified in the next sentence.

c *Nicht wahr?* (Isn't it?) can be added to most opinions and it is a good way to invite the other person to speak. It helps to make the conversation more natural.

d It's a good idea to vary your choice of words from time to time and an adjective such as *riesengroß* will attract more marks than simply *sehr groß*.

e An excellent sentence using *aber* to introduce some interesting information.

f This phrase *man sagt …* can often be used as another way to bring in an opinion. You could also use *Ich glaube, daß …* (I believe that …).

g *Es scheint auch, daß …* (It also seems that …) is an excellent way to vary the presentation of ideas and can be adapted to many situations.

h This is sure to score well – an opinion with a good justification using the construction *um … zu*, with the infinitive at the end, meaning: in order to …

i Turn the question round to your advantage by looking to the future, adding a new idea and keeping a positive tone to your conversation. This is an excellent technique to practise.

j Another high-scoring sentence, expressing an opinion and adding two reasons to back it up.

Speaking
Area A

3 Health and fitness

Rôle-play

A Foundation/Higher

- Prepare for this in just two minutes, including the time you need with a dictionary.

- Use all the information on the card to help you prepare.

- Note that you will be speaking to a dentist and should therefore use the *Sie* form of address. The teacher's introduction will usually make this clear to you by using the appropriate form of address for the situation.

BEIM ZAHNARZT

You are on holiday in Germany and have had terrible toothache for two days. You decide that you have to go and see a dentist. Your teacher will play the part of the dentist and will start the conversation.

Greet the dentist and say who you are. Say what the problem is. Answer the dentist's question. Ask if you have to pay anything.

1 Begrüße den Zahnarzt und sag, wer du bist.

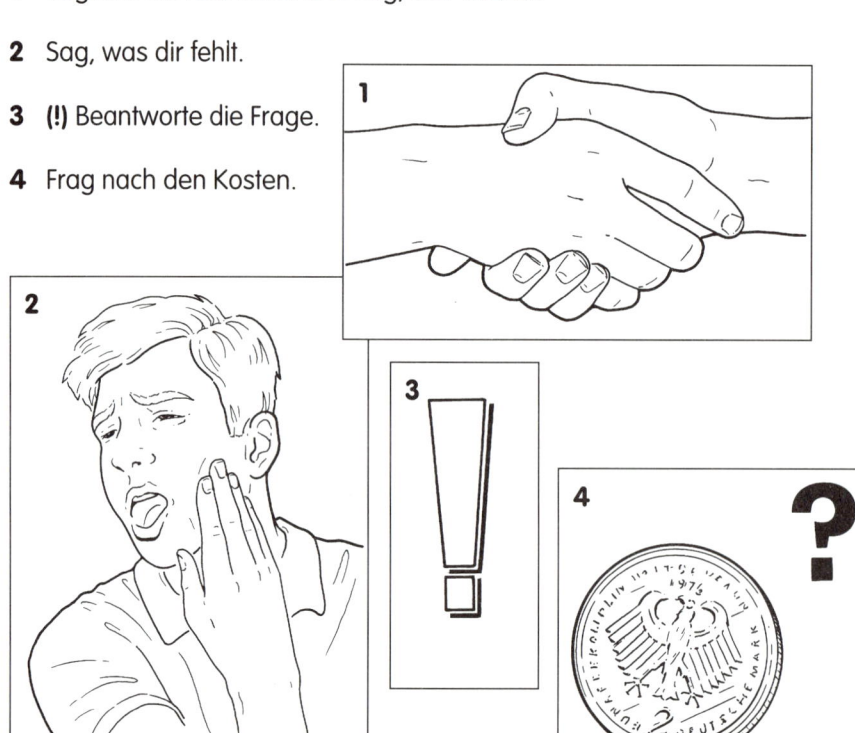

2 Sag, was dir fehlt.

3 (!) Beantworte die Frage.

4 Frag nach den Kosten.

(Solution: page 123)

B Higher

- With this type of Higher tier rôle-play you need to study **all** the information on the page very carefully, including any notices or announcements which may have been reproduced for you.

- Although there are only three prompts, you must remember that a Higher rôle-play is not rigidly structured and that the examiner will ask as many questions as are needed to get the information (s)he wants from you. Prepare by working out the things you may have to say:

  1. Greet the receptionist and say you want to see a doctor.
  2. Give your name.
  3. Say why you are calling.
  4. Describe your symptoms.
  5. Say you are going home tomorrow.
  6. Ask for or agree to an appointment.

- Be prepared for the unpredictable element. Here it might be to say where you are staying or what you are doing in Germany; spell your name; turn down an appointment for a day after your planned departure, etc.

- When you are ready, listen to the cassette and pause it to play your part before you hear the model answers. Then look at the solution and check your answers. Finally, work with the recording of the full rôle-play and learn your part.

BEIM ARZT

You are on holiday in Germany and are going home tomorrow. You are taken ill and telephone the doctor's receptionist. The Examiner will begin the conversation.

Dr. med. Norbert Puls

Arzt für Allgemeinmedizin

MO.–FR. 10.00–11.30 UND 16.00–18.00 Uhr

Tel. 61133

- **Persönliche Angaben**
- **Grund des Anrufs**
- **Symptome**

© London Examinations, a division of Edexcel Foundation 1996

(Solution: page 124)

Speaking
Area A

4 Food

Rôle-play

A Foundation

- Look at the first rôle-play that follows and begin to prepare yourself picture by picture.

  No. 1 Here you need to ask for a table for four. You can use *Haben Sie* or *Ich möchte …* If you really want to show off, you could say *Ich habe einen Tisch … reserviert*.

  No. 2 Order sausage …

  No. 3 … and chips.

  No. 4 You want a drink – ask for something like the drink in the picture to be on the safe side – lemonade or orange squash, for example.

  No. 5 The question mark tells you to ask a question, in this case where the toilets are.

- You now have two minutes to prepare, using a dictionary if you need to. You don't have time to look up many words, so keep it as simple as possible. You will get credit for Nos. 2–4 simply by providing the word for each item.

- Study the model answer. Then listen to it on the cassette, repeating after the actor, then with him/her and, finally, on your own (see page 56 *How to learn the model answers*). Note that your teacher will start the rôle-play, as per the instructions, so take your cue from the teacher.

- When you can perform this rôle-play easily, work on the next rôle-play. You have two minutes to prepare it. Then play the cassette and pause it to say your lines.

- When you have worked through the second rôle-play, look at the solution. Then listen to the recording again and repeat your rôle as you listen and try to learn it.

Speaking
Area A

1 IM RESTAURANT

Sie wollen mit Freunden essen.

You are in a German restaurant and you want to have a meal with friends. Your teacher will play the part of the waiter/waitress and will start the conversation.

Key words and phrases

Haben Sie (Do you have); *einen Tisch* (a table); *für vier Personen* (for four people); *Ich möchte* (I would like); *Bratwurst* (sausage); *bitte* (please); *Pommes frites* (Chips); *eine Limonade* (a lemonade); *Wo sind* (Where are); *die Toiletten* (the toilets).

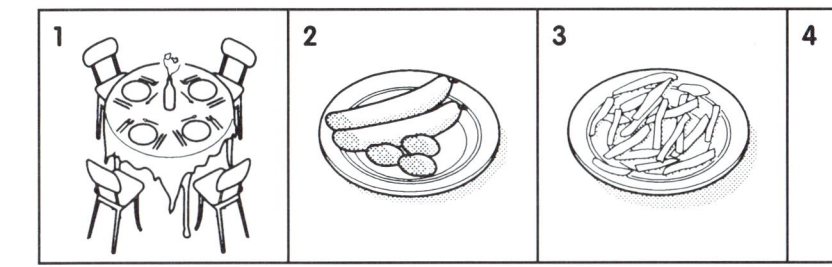

© MEG Specimen Papers 1997/8

(Solution: page 124)

2 IM CAFÉ

You are in a café in Germany with your parents. You order something to eat and drink. Your teacher will play the part of the waiter/waitress and will start the conversation.

Key words and phrases

Zwei Tassen Kaffee (two cups of coffee); *ein Glas Cola* (a glass of cola); *der Kuchen* (the cake); *drei Stück Kuchen* (three pieces of cake); *Was kostet das?* (How much is that?); *die Rechnung, bitte* (the bill, please); *Zahlen, bitte.* (I'd like to pay, please).

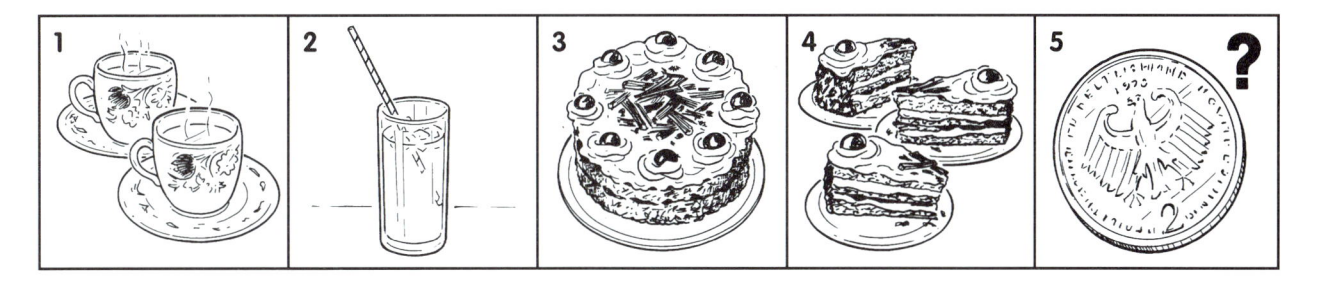

(Solution: page 125)

Speaking
Area A

B Foundation/Higher

◆ You have two minutes to prepare this rôle-play. Look at the pictures below and prepare your vocabulary and phrases.

◆ Try not to use a dictionary this time, but you would probably have time to look up two words at most, if you really need to.

No. 1 The English instructions tell you to ask for a table; the picture shows that you want a table for two.
No. 2 The exclamation mark means that you should expect a question from the examiner. Think of the sort of question a waiter might ask you after you have asked for a table for two.
No. 3 The English instructions tell you to ask for the menu – the picture reminds you of this.
No. 4 This picture reminds you of the English instructions: to order your meal. Ask for something to eat and drink.

◆ When you are ready, play the recording, pause it and speak your part. Then look at the solution and get your answers exactly right. Finally, work on the model recording and learn your lines.

IM RESTAURANT

You are in a restaurant in Berlin with a friend. You ask for a table, the menu and then order your meal. Remember to reply to the waiter/waitress's question. The Examiner will begin the conversation.

© London Examinations, a division of Edexcel Foundation 1996

(Solution: page 125)

Key words and phrases

Wo möchten Sie sitzen? (Where would you like to sit?); *hier in der Ecke* (here in the corner); *Kann ich ... haben?* (may I have ... ?); *die Speisekarte* (the menu); *wir möchten* (we would like); *zwei Cola* (two colas); *zwei Käsebrote* (two cheese sandwiches).

Speaking
Area A

Conversation

- In the conversation part of your speaking test, your teacher will ask a series of questions. Try, however, not to rely on these questions all the time and show some initiative of your own. You could, for example, ask questions of your own, to make it more like a real conversation.

- You can't prepare for the conversation on the day of the exam, as you won't know what the topics are. So make sure that you practise a lot in the year leading up to the exam.

- Practise answering these popular exam questions about food. Work on your own with the book and cassette and also, if you can, with a partner (see page 56 *How to learn the model answers*).

A Foundation

1 Was trinkst du gern?

2 Was ißt du gern?

3 Was ißt du zum Frühstück?

4 Wo ißt du normalerweise zu Mittag?

5 Gefällt dir das, oder?

(Solution: page 126)

B Foundation/Higher

- Remember that you must refer to the past, present and future, and express some opinions to achieve a grade C. Always be on the look-out for the chance to say such things as:
  – *Letzte Woche, zum Beispiel, habe ich …*
  – *Nächsten Samstag, zum Beispiel, gehe ich …*
  – *Meiner Meinung nach …*

1 Warst du schon in Deutschland?

2 Was ist ein typisch deutsches Essen, deiner Meinung nach?

3 Was wirst du heute abend essen?

4 Beschreib bitte dein ideales Essen.

5 „Yorkshire Pudding" – was ist das genau?

(Solutions: page 126)

Speaking
Area A

C Higher

- To earn good marks here you **must** refer to past, present and future and express and justify your personal opinions.

- You need to take the initiative whenever you can and develop the conversation: don't just give short answers to your teacher's questions.

- Remember to try other techniques such as:

    Nein, … aber/Zum Beispiel …/Weil …

- Now look at the model answer. Listen to the recording and repeat the answers, after, with and without the recording (see page 56 *How to learn the model answers*).

- Think of as many ways as possible of replacing the underlined words. Then play the recording and answer all the questions by pausing it, without looking at your book.

1 Was würdest du sagen, wenn ich dir Sauerkraut zu essen gäbe?

2 Welche Gerichte kochst du selbst gern?

3 Sag mir, wie man einen Tisch decken sollte.

4 Was für ein Essen würdest du vorschlagen, wenn du einen deutschen Freund zu Besuch hättest?

5 Was ist dein Lieblingsrestaurant?

(Solution: page 127)

Speaking
Area B

B Personal and social life

1 Self, family and friends

Conversation

- People often talk about themselves, their families and their friends in real life and in exams. You can learn how to hold a conversation on this important topic.

- First of all study the questions. Make sure that you understand them. Then practice listening to them to be sure that you recognise each question as soon as you hear it. Listen as many times as you need to until you can hear and understand every question without delay.

- Then work on the answers for the tier you are preparing, using the book and the cassette (see page 56 *How to learn the model answers*). You will see how the same questions can be answered in different ways. Your aim is to have an excellent answer for each question. If you can, get a partner to ask you all the questions several times, changing the order of the questions each time.

- Look at the answers, adapting the underlined words to make them your answer.

Foundation (A) and Higher (B)

1 Erzähl mir etwas von deiner Familie.

2 Was für Geschwister hast du?

3 Was ist dein Lieblingshaustier?

4 Wann hast du Geburtstag?

5 Kannst du deinen besten Freund oder deine beste Freundin beschreiben?

(Solutions: page 128)

Speaking
Area B

2 Free time, holidays and special occasions

Rôle-play

A Foundation/Higher

- Use the instructions to prepare for this rôle-play.
- Plan to keep your answers short and simple, because no extra marks are given for longer responses in rôle-plays.
- This rôle-play is with a friend, so you must use the *du* form.
- Look out for the second question, which is an unpredictable element. Note that you are also required to explain your response. Try to think what question you might be asked – it is most likely to be whether you have seen or like a certain film or type of film. Think too about a reason and try to use *weil* with the verb at the end. The last question mentions Wales. Unless you live there, you should replace it with your own country or town.
- After two minutes of preparation, play the tape, pause it and say your answers. You can then play on and hear the rôle-play being acted out for you. Learn your lines by repeating them, after and with the recording. Then, if you can, act out the rôle-play with a partner, taking turns to play each part.
- The solution gives some other possible answers. As you practise with your partner you could try saying these too. It is worth bearing in mind that every variation you learn may come up in the listening exam or could possibly be used to your advantage in the writing exam.

You are with your German pen-friend in Germany. You talk about the weekend. Your pen-friend begins.

1 Frag über Filme im Kino am Samstag.
2 Beantworte die Frage und sag warum!
3 Erklär, was du am Sonntag machen möchtest.
4 Sag, wann du am Sonntag aufstehst.
5 Beschreib etwas, was ihr am Wochenende in Wales macht.

© Welsh Joint Education Committee 1995

(Solution: page 129)

Key words and phrases

Was läuft im Kino? (What's on at the cinema?); *weil ich diesen Film nicht gesehen habe* (because I haven't seen this film); *gegen neun* (about nine o'clock); *Wie wär's mit ...* (How about ...); *um Kaffee zu trinken* ((in order) to drink coffee).

B Foundation/Higher

🔸 Study the instructions and visuals closely for two minutes.

🔸 Think carefully about the second response. You are going to the sports centre so it could be about your favourite sport, or when/where you play at home. It won't be a 'yes/no' question such as 'Have you got your trainers?' so be ready to listen and think carefully before you answer.

BEI EINER FAMILIE

You are staying with your German exchange partner. You are arranging to go out with him/her to a sports centre and you also want to know if you can eat there. The Examiner will begin the conversation.

© London Examinations, a division of Edexcel Foundation 1996

(Solution: page 129)

Conversation

🔸 It is very important to remember that most of the German you use in letters can also be used in conversations. If you can, look at pages 78–79 and 110–111 in *Revise for German GCSE Reading and Writing*: think how you could use what you learnt there to answer the questions below.

🔸 Then listen to the cassette and you will hear some model answers. To help you learn them you could listen to the answers and write them down. Listen as many times as you need to. Keep the answers safe and use them for revision before your exam.

A Foundation

1 Wenn du keine Schulaufgaben hast, was machst du gern?

2 Wieviel Taschengeld bekommst du?

3 Wofür gibst du dein Taschengeld aus?

4 Sparst du dein Geld?

5 Hast du einen Job, um Geld zu verdienen?

B Foundation/Higher

1 Was hast du letztes Wochenende gemacht?

2 Was hast du nach den Examen vor?

3 Wo verbringst du deine Sommerferien dieses Jahr?

4 Mit wem gehst du gern aus?

C Higher

1 Wenn du nach Deutschland fahren könntest, was möchtest du da machen?

2 Was machst du am liebsten in deiner Freizeit?

3 Bekommst du deiner Meinung nach genug Taschengeld?

4 Erzähl mir von einem Film, den du neulich gesehen hast.

(Solutions: pages 129–131)

3 Arranging a meeting or activity

Rôle-play

- Allow yourself five minutes to prepare both the Foundation/Higher tier and the Higher tier rôle-plays. For the first one, you need to study the English instructions very carefully and make sure you understand the German text stimulus as well as the four brief cues. You may need to look up a word or two in your dictionary.

- Most exam boards make the teacher start the rôle-play, but for some you may need to take the initiative. Here you should start with a question about going out with your friend. Play the recording, pause it and say your responses before the actor. Then look at the transcript and practise speaking after the actor, then with him/her. When you are confident, use only the rôle-play on page 79 as your cue to speak in the recording.

Speaking
Area B

A Foundation/Higher

You are staying with your friend in Germany. You want to arrange to go out one evening. Agree with your friend (your teacher) where you will go and on what day. Fix a time and place to meet also. You have your diary – make sure you check when you are free!

1 Wohin?

2 An welchem Tag?

3 Wo?

4 Um wieviel Uhr?

Mo 11. Juni	
Schule 8.00–12.30	17.00 Schwimmen
Di 12. Juni	
Schule 8.00–13.25	Volleyball, 18.00–20.00
Mi 13. Juni	
Schule 9.00–13.25	15.00 Kegeln
Do 14. Juni	
Schule 8.00–14.20	
Frei 15. Juni	
Schule 8.00–13.25	Disco, 20.00–23.00

© Northern Examinations & Assessment Board 1996

Key words and phrases

Könnten wir …? (Could we …?); *Das wäre schön* (That would be nice); *Geht das?* (Is that all right?); *Ach, schade* (Oh, what a shame); *Ich habe versprochen* (I've promised); *Gute Idee* (Good idea); *Das ist mir egal* (I don't mind).

B Higher

◊ The text stimulus is very important as well as the three cues in German. Try to think of the kinds of activities you could do at a *Freizeitzentrum*. What could you take with you for a whole day's visit? When and where will you meet your friend? Be ready too, for the unexpected question, which will probably link to one of the phrases in the text.

FREIZEITZENTRUM
Kirchdorf
FREIBAD
SCHNELLIMBISS
SPIEL UND SPASS
Täglich 10.00 bis 19.00 Uhr

■ Aktivitäten
■ Was einpacken?
■ Treffpunkt

You are on holiday in Germany and you see this advertisement. You telephone your German friend in order to arrange a day out there. The examiner will begin the conversation.

© London Examinations, a division of Edexcel Foundation 1996

Key words and phrases

Ich habe einen Vorschlag (I've a suggestion); *Es macht Spaß … zu …* (It's fun to …); *von zehn bis neunzehn Uhr* (from ten 'til seven o'clock).

(Solutions: page 131)

Speaking
Area B

4 Leisure and entertainment
Rôle-play

> Study the rôle-plays below, choosing the two for the exam tier you are entering. Your responses have been included this time. To help you learn them you could:
>
> 1 Read them silently and aloud.
> 2 Listen to the recording once, then listen again and repeat.
> 3 Look at a question, cover the answer and try to say the answer.
> 4 Listen to a question and try to say the answer before listening to it on the recording.
> 5 Listen once more and try to say all the alternatives suggested in the notes.

A Foundation

You are talking with your German friend at home about what there is to do.

1 You need to tell him/her there is a cinema and a swimming pool.
2 You want to say that you like swimming a lot.
3 You need to find out what he/she wants to do tomorrow.
4 You decide to accept his/her suggestion.

Model answers

Lehrer: Du bist zu Hause in England, ich bin dein deutscher Gast. Was gibt es hier in der Stadt zu tun?
Du: **Es gibt ᵃ ein Kino und ein Schwimmbad.**
Lehrer: Gehst du oft dahin?
Du: **Ja, ich schwimme sehr gern. ᵇ**
Lehrer: Ich auch.
Du: **Was möchtest du morgen machen?**
Lehrer: Ich möchte die Stadt besichtigen.
Du: **Ja, gute Idee! ᶜ**

> **a** You could also use *wir haben* here.
>
> **b** *Ich gehe gern schwimmen* is an alternative answer.
>
> **c** There are many ways to accept a suggestion: *Ja, warum nicht; Ja, machen wir das; Toll, die Stadt ist sehr interessant.; Prima, dann treffen wir uns mit unseren Freunden im Eiscafé; Ach, die Stadt ist langweilig, wollen wir nicht lieber Radfahren gehen?*

Key words and phrases

das Schwimmbad (swimming pool); *ich schwimme sehr gern* (I really like swimming); *Ich möchte* (I'd like); *gute Idee* (good idea).

Speaking
Area B

B Foundation/Higher

You are staying with a German family. You intend to go out tomorrow night with a friend to see a film in town. The film finishes at 10.45 pm. Your teacher will play the part of your host and will start the conversation.

Model answers

Lehrer: Wir sind bei mir in Deutschland.
Was willst du morgen abend machen?
Du: **Ich gehe ins Kino in der Stadt.**
Lehrer: Und wie kommst du dahin? [a]
Du: **Mit dem Bus. Nach dem Film nehmen wir ein Taxi.** [b]
Lehrer: Und mit wem gehst du?
Du: **Mit einer Freundin.** [c]
Lehrer: O.K., aber du mußt vor halb elf zu Hause sein.
Du: **Aber das ist nicht möglich** [d]**, der Film ist erst um Viertel vor elf aus.**
Lehrer: Ach so. Dann sagen wir spätestens Viertel nach elf.
Du: **Gut, einverstanden.** [e] **Danke.**

a This type of unprepared question must appear in every rôle-play for the Foundation/Higher tier, so be ready for it. Most exam boards signal its appearance with a symbol such as '**!**'. You have to listen carefully and make any appropriate response.

b The choice of transport is entirely yours. Choose a phrase you are confident with. Other possibilities are: *Zu Fuß./Meine Freundin kommt mit ihrem Vater im Auto./Mit der Straßenbahn.*

c You may say: *Mit einem Freund, Karl* or *Mit Freunden.*

d Another answer could be: *Aber, das kann ich nicht.*

e This is a useful word meaning 'agreed'. It can be used to accept a suggestion or an order.

Key words and phrases

Wir nehmen ein Taxi (we're taking a taxi); *mit einer Freundin* or *mit einem Freund* (with a friend); *nicht möglich* (not possible); *einverstanden* (agreed).

Speaking
Area B

C Higher

You are staying with a friend in Germany. You discuss what you can do tonight. You would like to go to the cinema and ask for a newspaper to find out what is on. You will need to find out what your friend recommends.

Model answers

Lehrer: Wir sind bei mir in Deutschland. Was machen wir heute abend?

Du: **Ich möchte ins Kino gehen. Was für Filme siehst du gern?** a

Lehrer: Meistens Komödien. Wie oft gehst du ins Kino in England?

Du: **Ach, vielleicht zweimal im Monat.** b

Lehrer: Und was sind deine Lieblingsfilme?

Du: **Ich sehe am liebsten Krimis oder Abenteuerfilme. Wo ist die Zeitung, bitte? Ich gucke, was heute läuft.** c

Lehrer: Hier ist sie.

Du: **Danke. Also, was schlägst du vor?** d

Lehrer: Vielleicht „Tod in Afrika".

Du: **Gut, einverstanden.**

a This phrase *Was für ...* followed by the accusative case is a useful way to ask about what kind/sort of thing.

b A good response to the unprepared question. You could have said *Jede Woche* (every week); *jeden Samstagabend* (every Saturday evening) or even *Nur, wenn etwas Gutes läuft.* (Only when there's something good on.)

c *Ich gucke* (I'll look) is a useful phrase. You'll often hear the verb used in this form *Guck mal!* (look!).

d *Was würdest du empfehlen?* (What would you recommend?) is another possibility here. *Was schlägst du vor?* (What do you suggest?)

Key words and phrases

Ich sehe am liebsten Krimis oder Abenteuerfilme (or whatever other kind of film you like.)

Speaking
Area B

PRACTISING UNDER EXAM CONDITIONS

> When you have learnt the model rôle-plays, work on one of those below. Do this as if you were in the exam:
> 1 Give yourself just two minutes to prepare.
> 2 Listen to the cassette and say your part in the pauses.

Rôle-play

A Foundation

You are in a café with a German friend talking about your plans for the evening. Your teacher will play the part of your friend and will speak first.

1 You need to ask your friend what (s)he is doing this evening.

2 You want to suggest going to the cinema.

3 You need to know what time the film starts.

4 You want to say that you will see her/him soon.

1	2	3	4
Heute abend?	KINO KINO ?	clock ?	wave goodbye

B Higher

You are telephoning a German friend to arrange a visit to the cinema. You need to agree on a choice of film and explain why you choose it. Your teacher will speak first.

1 Name. Kino vorschlagen. Wann?

2 Welchen Film?

3 Wähl einen Film. Warum diesen Film?

4 Treffpunkt – wann und wo?

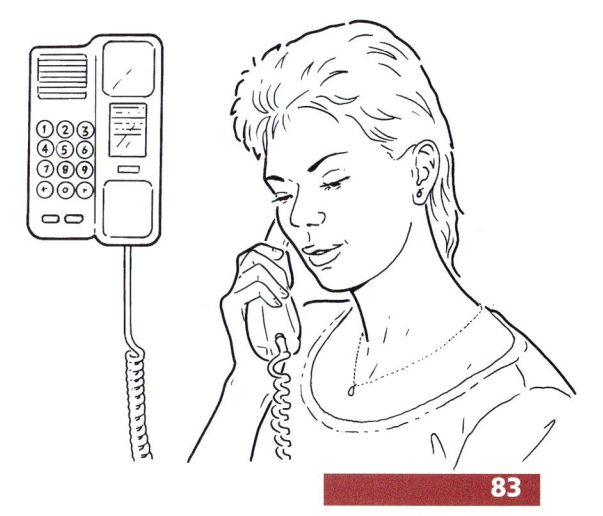

(Solutions: page 132)

Speaking
Area C

C The world around us

1 Home town, local environment and customs

Conversation

- In the conversation part of your exam your teacher will do everything possible to get you to refer to past, present and future events as well as to express personal opinions.
- If you are aiming at Grades A*–C, work on all the questions.
- When you have thought about your answers, listen to the cassette. To help you to learn the model answers you could:
  1. Listen to them several times and look at them in the Solutions.
  2. Repeat them, first with the Solutions and then without looking at them.
  3. Listen to the model answers and write them down.
  4. Adapt these answers to match your town, region and opinions.

  You will then be ready to talk about this section in your exam.

A Foundation

1. **Beschreib die Stadt, in der du wohnst.**
   (This is a very open question and gives you the chance to say anything you know, e.g. Where it is, what there is to see and do there, what you think of it.)

2. **Und was gibt es dort für Teenager?**
   (This offers an excellent opportunity to say what there is, what you did last weekend, what you intend to do next Saturday and to express an opinion.)

3. **Wie kommst du von deinem Haus zur Stadtmitte? Fährst du mit dem Bus, oder?**
   (A good chance to say what you usually do and even what you did last Sunday.)

4. **Und wie ist das Wetter dort im Winter?**
   (Another excellent opportunity to say what it usually is like and compare it with last year.)

5. **Also wohnst du gern dort?**
   (Another chance to give an opinion and to ask what your teacher thinks.)

B Higher

1 Seit wann wohnst du dort?
   (This allows you to use *'seit'* with a present tense in your answer. Also say where else you may have lived and which you prefer and why.)

2 Wenn du viel Geld hättest, wo würdest du gerne wohnen?
   (You can now refer to the future and express more opinions.)

3 Was sollte man in deiner Stadt für die Jugendlichen tun?
   (Try here to refer to the past, present and future.)

4 Beschreib eine Stadt oder eine Gegend in Deutschland.
   (A town you've visited or read about. Don't forget the **Nein, aber** … approach.)

5 Weißt du die Wettervorhersage für morgen?
   (You can refer to the future and express more opinions.)

(Solutions: page 133)

2 Finding the way

Rôle-play

- When marking your rôle-plays, the examiner will give you full marks if each message is conveyed, even if you make mistakes. Concentrate on this – make sure a German speaker can understand it.

- Look at both the rôle-plays on page 86 and prepare to act them out. You have three minutes to prepare them.

- Then listen to the cassette, pause it and say your part before the actor.

- Remember to speak clearly and to get your message across. If you are not happy with your first attempt, do it a second time and try to improve. Then listen to the model version all the way through. Listen to it several times, firstly as you look at the solution and then without it. Write a note of anything in it which you wish you had said.

- When you think you are ready to play these rôles perfectly, you could:

  1 play them again, pausing in the middle of **your** messages and trying to complete them before playing on and listening;

  2 pause before each of your messages and try to say each one before listening to it again.

Speaking
Area C

A Foundation

You want to catch a train in Germany.

1. You need to ask someone where the station is.
2. You need to know how far it is.
3. You want to find out if there is a bus.
4. You should say thank you and good-bye.

Your teacher will play the part of a passer-by and will speak first.

Key words and phrases

Entschuldigen Sie, bitte (Excuse me, please); *Ist es weit von hier?* (Is it far from here?).

B Foundation/Higher

In your home town a German-speaking tourist stops you and asks you the way. Give directions. Your teacher will play the part of the tourist and will speak first.

Key words and phrases

Gehen Sie hier geradeaus (Go straight on); *über die Brücke* (over the bridge); *Nehmen Sie die erste/zweite/dritte Straße links/rechts.* (Take the first/second/third/street on the left/right.)

(Solutions: page 134)

3 Shopping

Rôle-play

- Choose **A** and **B** if you are aiming for a grade C, or **B** and **C** if you are aiming for grades A* to C. Give yourself four minutes to prepare the two rôle-plays, using a dictionary to check on a few words if you need to. Remember, however, only to look up words if it is absolutely necessary.
  1. In **A** and **B** you can choose which items to buy, so ask for two things that you already know.
  2. In **C** you can choose what your problem purchase was and what is wrong with it, as well as suggesting a solution, so base your preparation on using what you already know.

- When you feel confident, look at the answers and listen to the conversations all the way through. Use the answers and the recordings to help you learn your lines (see page 56 *How to learn the model answers*).

Speaking
Area C

A Foundation

ANDENKEN

You are buying presents and need to buy two items. Remember to greet the shopkeeper and end the conversation politely.

© London Examinations, a division of Edexcel Foundation 1996

> **Key words and phrases**
>
> *Ich möchte ...* (I'd like ...); *Was kostet das, bitte?* (How much is it, please?)

B Foundation/Higher

You are at a campsite shop to buy food for a picnic. Your teacher will play the part of the shop assistant and will speak first.

1 Sie wollen zwei Sachen zu essen.

2 Sie wollen auch Obst – sagen Sie, was für Obst Sie wollen.

3 Sie brauchen auch etwas zu trinken.

4 (!!) Zahlen Sie, und beantworten Sie die Frage.

C Higher

You are on holiday in Germany and have bought a present to take back home for someone in your family. When you get back to your holiday house you find there is something wrong with the present. You take it back to the shop to complain. Your teacher will play the part of the shop assistant, but you must start the conversation.

1 Geschenk ... Für wen?   2 Problem?   3 Lösung?

> **Key words and phrases**
>
> *Es hat ein kleines Loch* (It's got a little hole); *Gegen halb elf* (At about half past ten); *Können Sie es umtauschen?* (Can you change it?)

(Solutions: pages 135–136)

Speaking
Area C

4 Public services

Rôle-play

> Think of what you would have to say in the following situations and what questions you would have to answer. If you feel confident, act out your rôle with the recording, pausing the cassette to say your lines before listening to the model answers. Then use the Solutions to learn your lines. Finally try to work with a partner and take turns to act the different parts.

A Foundation

You are at the post office in Germany. You have three post cards to send home. You only have a fifty Mark note.

Your teacher will play the part of the post office clerk and will speak first.

1. You need to ask how much it costs for a post card to England.
2. You need to buy three stamps for 80 Pfennig.
3. You want to apologise for only having 50 DM.
4. You want to thank the clerk and say good-bye.

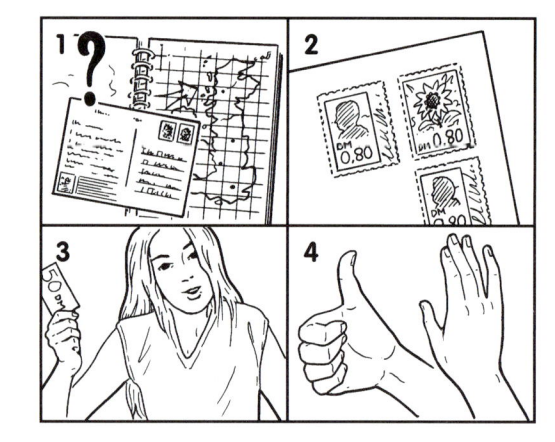

Key words and phrases

Was kostet . . . ? (How much is . . .?); *X Briefmarken zu X Pfennig* (X stamps at X pence); *Es tut mir leid* (I'm sorry); Note the use of *Stück* for a coin, too e.g. *Ein Zwanzigpfennigstück* (A 20 pence piece).

B Foundation/Higher

IN DER BANK

You go into a German bank. You have no German money left, but you have travellers' cheques to change. Your teacher will play the part of the bank employee and will start the conversation.

1. Sie haben einige Reiseschecks. Was sagen Sie?
2. Sagen Sie, wie viele und was für Reiseschecks Sie haben.
3. Beantworten Sie die Frage.
4. Sie haben Ihren Paß nicht dabei. Sagen Sie, wo der Paß ist.
5. Fragen Sie nach den Öffnungszeiten der Bank.

© MEG Specimen Papers 1997/8

(Solutions: page 136)

C Higher

Sie sind im Fundbüro in Deutschland. Sie haben einen Fotoapparat im Einkaufszentrum verloren. Ihr Lehrer beginnt die Unterhaltung.

1. Hat man ihn gefunden?
2. Beantworten Sie die Fragen von dem Angestellten, zum Beispiel: Wo? Wann? Was für einen?

(Solution: page 137)

5 Getting around

Rôle-play

- Choose two of the rôle-plays below and give yourself three minutes to prepare them.

- Remember, with Foundation/Higher and Higher tiers, you will always have something unexpected to cope with. Usually it will be the sort of thing that happens in those situations in real life. Think of some of the things that might happen and, with practice, you can learn how to prepare for this.

- One way of coping with problems is to ask:
  - *Gibt es eine andere Tankstelle (Post, Jugendherberge, Bäckerei, usw.) hier in der Nähe?*
  - *Gibt es einen anderen Supermarkt (Markt, Bahnhof, Campingplatz, usw.) hier in der Nähe?*
  - *Gibt es ein anderes Geschäft (Hotel, Kaufhaus, Museum, usw.) hier in der Nähe?*

- If you feel confident, listen to the cassette, pause it and play your part before listening to the model answers.

- Use the solutions and the recording to learn your lines. Work with a partner and take turns to act both rôles.

A Foundation

AM BAHNHOF
Sie wollen mit dem Zug fahren.

You are at the railway station in Germany and want to travel by train. Your teacher will play the part of the booking clerk and will start the conversation.

1	2	3	4	5
→ BONN ?	So. **Mo.** Di.	16:20	2 A BONN	?

© MEG Specimen Papers 1997/8

(Solution: page 137)

Speaking
Area C

B Foundation/Higher

AM BAHNHOF

You are at the ticket office in a station in Germany and want to travel to Bonn by train. You also want to know if you have to reserve and where somewhere else is in the station. You speak to the ticket office clerk. The Examiner will begin the conversation.

| 1 ⇌/→ | 2 ! | 3 R? | 4 👫/🍴/i? |

© London Examinations, a division of Edexcel Foundation 1996

Key words and phrases

Einmal/zweimal/viermal nach Köln (One/two/four tickets to Cologne); *Einfach/hin und zürück* (Single/return); *Wann fährt der Zug/der Bus?* (What time does the train/bus leave?); *Wann kommt der Zug in Bonn an?* (What time does the train arrive in Bonn?)

C Higher

You are at a service station, buying fuel for your family car.

Your teacher will play the part of the attendant and will start the conversation.

Key words and phrases

Ich möchte dreißig Liter Bleifrei, bitte. (I'd like thirty litres of lead-free petrol, please.); *Geben Sie mir für fünfzig Mark Super, bitte.* (Give me fifty marks worth of super, please.); *Könnten Sie die Reifen prüfen, bitte?* (Could you check the tyres, please?)

(Solutions: page 138)

Speaking
Area D

D The **world** of **work**

1 Education and training

Conversation

- This is a topic which often comes up in the conversation. So make sure that you are ready for it!

- Begin by studying the questions below on the left, while covering the model answers on the right. Make sure that you can easily understand the questions when you hear them.

- When you are confident that you can understand the questions as soon as you hear them, look at some possible answers on the right. Change the words underlined to give you the answers you want.

- Now listen to a recording of a very good candidate answering these questions and try to base your answers on his. Then play the recording of each question again, pause it and practise giving your own answers.

Foundation/Higher

Questions	Model answers
1 Was wirst du nach deinen Prüfungen machen?	Nach meinen Prüfungen hoffe ich, in die Oberstufe zu gehen/ hier in der Schule zu bleiben/eine Arbeitsstelle zu kriegen/mich auf das Abitur vorzubereiten. Ich möchte Englisch, Deutsch und Geschichte machen.
2 Was möchtest du später einmal machen?	Ich möchte auf die Universität gehen, um Naturwissenschaften zu studieren. Ich möchte in einem Büro/in einem Geschäft/in einer Fabrik arbeiten. Ich möchte Lehrerin/Mechaniker/Arzt/Tierarzt/Kindergärtnerin werden. Ich möchte auf die Uni gehen, um Zahnarzt/Architekt/Ingenieurin zu werden.
3 Warum willst du das machen?	Weil ich Naturwissenschaften sehr interessant finde. Weil ich Geld verdienen möchte/diese Arbeit sehr interessant finde/sehr gern studiere und das Studentenleben toll sein soll.
4 Was hältst du von deiner Schule?	Meistens war sie gut. Geschichte habe ich besonders gut gefunden. *Give your own favourite subject, e.g.* Physik/Erdkunde/Mathe/Informatik/Französisch.

91

Speaking
Area D

2 Careers and employment

Rôle-play

Foundation/Higher

> - Study the rôle-play below. Give yourself three minutes to prepare for it.
> - Then see the model answer below for the way this rôle-play could be done. To learn to do this, follow the steps given on page 80.

AM TELEFON

You are looking for work in Germany. You speak on the phone with a manager. Your teacher will play the part of the manager and will start the conversation.

1 Sagen Sie, wie Sie heißen, und woher Sie kommen.

2 Beantworten Sie die Frage.

3 Sagen Sie, was für einen Job Sie schon gehabt haben.

4 Sagen Sie, für wie lange Sie arbeiten möchten.

5 Fragen Sie nach Unterkunft.

© MEG Specimen Papers 1997/8

a Of course, you might say *aus England/Wales/Nordirland/Irland*.

b You can adjust the time, *seit zwei/drei/vier/Jahren*.

c Other job possibilities are: *Ich arbeite als Kellner/Kellnerin in einem Café./Ich bin Verkäufer./Verkäuferin in einem großen Warenhaus./Ich helfe meiner Mutter im Geschäft.* Or you may need to say: *Ich habe keinen Job, aber ich möchte in einem Hotel arbeiten. Zwei von meinen Freunden machen das am Wochenende.*

d Another good answer would be: *Ich kann sofort anfangen und möchte bis zum Ende der Sommerferien arbeiten.* (I can start straightaway and would like to work until the end of the summer holidays.)

e You could ask: *Wie sind die Unterkunftmöglichkeiten, bitte?* (What are the possibilities for accommodation, please?)

Model answers

Lehrer: Sie suchen Arbeit in Deutschland. Sie sprechen mit einer Managerin.

Hallo. Frau Gerling am Apparat. Kann ich Ihnen helfen? Sie suchen Arbeit in Deutschland, ja? Wie heißen Sie und woher kommen Sie?

Du: **Hallo. Ich heiße Graham Struthers. Ich komme aus Schottland.** ᵃ

Lehrer: Sie sprechen sehr gut Deutsch. Wie lange lernen Sie schon Deutsch?

Du: **Ich lerne seit fünf Jahren Deutsch.** ᵇ

Lehrer: Haben Sie schon einen Job gehabt?

Du: **Ja. Ich trage Zeitungen aus, und ich arbeite samstags in dem Zeitungsgeschäft.** ᶜ

Lehrer: Für wie lange möchten Sie arbeiten?

Du: **Für vier Wochen, wenn möglich.** ᵈ

Lehrer: Ich habe eine Stelle für Sie auf meinem Campingplatz. Brauchen Sie weitere Auskunft?

Du: **Ja. Wo kann ich wohnen?** ᵉ

Lehrer: Es gibt einen Wohnwagen auf meinem Campingplatz.

Du: **Ach, danke schön.**

Speaking
Area D

Conversation

- In your exam, you will take part in just one conversation with your teacher. Your teacher will begin with fairly easy questions and will gradually move on to questions which give you the opportunity to show off just how much you know and can do.

- Give yourself two minutes to study the questions below on the left, while covering the answers on the right. Start with the Foundation questions and move on to the Higher questions on page 94. Make sure that you understand them all. Look out for opportunities to give answers which express opinions and which refer to past, present and future. That's how you will get top marks. Say as much as you can and try to avoid long pauses.

- Now look at some possible answers to those questions on the right. **This is not on the cassette.** Learn any you could use in an exam to talk about yourself. Then adapt the others so that you could use them.

- Ask your teacher to correct your answers, then learn and practise them on your own and with a friend.

A Foundation

	Questions	Model answers
1	Hast du einen Job, um Geld zu verdienen?	Ja, ich arbeite, weil ich Geld zum Ausgeben brauche. Das macht auch Spaß.
2	Wo arbeitest du?	Ich arbeite im Supermarkt am Stadtrand.
3	Wann arbeitest du?	Also, normalerweise arbeite ich samstags und sonntags, aber letztes Wochenende habe ich nicht gearbeitet, weil ich diese Prüfung vorbereiten mußte.
4	Was ist dein Stundenlohn?	Nicht sehr viel. Ich bekomme nur drei Pfund die Stunde.
5	Was machst du mit dem Geld, das du verdienst?	Ich spare für die Ferien. Ich fahre dieses Jahr mit meinen Freunden nach Spanien in Urlaub.
6	Wie kommst du zur Arbeit?	Ich fahre mit dem Rad, oder, wenn das Wetter sehr schlecht ist, kann ich einen Bus nehmen.
7	Erzähl mir von einem normalen Arbeitstag.	Also, ich komme um halb neun an. Ich gehe sofort an die Kasse, wo ich den Kunden helfe, die Lebensmittel einzupacken, oder an der Kasse arbeite. Ich habe eine Stunde Mittagspause, und dann arbeite ich bis sechs Uhr weiter.
8	Gefällt dir deine Arbeit? Warum?	Nein, nicht besonders. Es ist langweilig, und die Kunden sind manchmal gemein. Ich hoffe, nach den Examen etwas Besseres zu finden.

Speaking
Area D

B Higher

Questions	Model answers
1 Wie hast du deinen Job gefunden?	Meine Eltern kaufen dort ein und haben ein Stellenangebot im Geschäft gesehen.
2 Seit wann arbeitest du dort?	Seit einem Jahr. Ich habe letzten Juli angefangen.
3 Was sind die Vor- und Nachteile von deinem Job?	Also, der Vorteil ist natürlich das Geld, weil ich mit meinen Freunden in Urlaub fahren kann. Der größte Nachteil ist, daß mein ganzes Wochenende nur aus Arbeit besteht, und ich keine Zeit habe, auszugehen.
4 Was sind deine Eltern von Beruf?	Meine Mutter ist Grundschullehrerin und mein Vater arbeitet bei einer Computerfirma. Ich finde, daß sie sehr schwer arbeiten müssen. Sie verlassen das Haus um acht Uhr und kommen erst gegen sechs Uhr zurück.
5 Was möchtest du als Beruf machen?	Also, ich weiß nicht genau. Ich hoffe, Zahnarzt zu werden, aber das ist gar nicht einfach.
6 Was für eine Ausbildung braucht man, um das zu machen?	Man muß auf die Uni gehen und dann, glaube ich, in einem Krankenhaus arbeiten. Die Ausbildung dauert sechs oder sieben Jahre. Ich weiß nicht, ob ich so lange warten könnte, bevor ich anfange, Geld zu verdienen.
7 Möchtest du im Ausland arbeiten? Wo? Warum?	Ja, ich möchte in Deutschland arbeiten. Vielleicht könnte ich das Jahr, bevor ich an die Uni gehe, in Berlin verbringen. Das ist eine tolle Stadt, habe ich gehört.
8 Was würdest du machen, wenn du keine Arbeit finden könntest?	Ich würde bei dem Chef von einem Supermarkt anrufen, um zu fragen, ob sie etwas für mich haben – genauso, wie ich es letztes Jahr gemacht habe.

◘ Before leaving this, look again at that conversation and try to find out why the candidate scored top marks.

1 Find three opinions which are justified.
2 Find three references to the past.
3 Find three references to the present.
4 Find three references to the future.

Key words and phrases

Es war langweilig, weil ich nicht viel zu tun hatte. (It was boring because I didn't have much to do.); *Die Leute waren unsympathisch* (The people weren't nice); *Die Arbeit war sehr schwer und ich war sehr müde am Abend.* (The work was very hard and I was very tired in the evening.); *Ich würde sehr gerne so eine Stelle haben, wenn ich die Schule verlasse.* (I would really like a job like that when I leave school.)

(Solutions: pages 138–139)

Speaking
Area D

PRACTISING UNDER EXAM CONDITIONS

- When you are confident that you can do the rôle-play and conversation on careers and employment, work on those below. Choose the two rôle-plays and the two conversations for the exam tier you are entering – Foundation and Foundation/Higher, or Foundation/Higher and Higher. Give yourself ten minutes to prepare and then give your answers.

- Then look at the model answers and listen to them on the recording. To learn them, you could follow the steps given on page 80.

- Remember to impress the examiner: try to say some interesting things and to be as fluent as possible. Sound as German as you can. Listening to the recording will help with this.

Rôle-play

A Foundation

You are in Germany on a work experience placement and staying with a German family. Your penfriend's father/mother asks you about your work. Your teacher will play the part of the father/mother and will speak first.

(Solution: page 139)

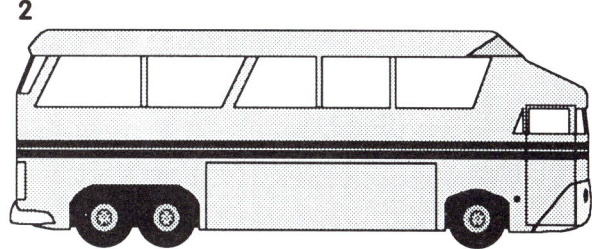

© Northern Examinations & Assessment Board 1996

Speaking
Area D

B Foundation/Higher

DAS INTERVIEW

You want to work in a restaurant in Freiburg. You go to a restaurant where a job has been advertised. Your teacher will play the part of the restaurant owner who is interviewing you for the job. S/he will start the conversation.

1. Stellen Sie sich vor, und sagen Sie, warum Sie da sind.
2. Geben Sie Ihr Alter und Ihre Nationalität an.
3. Geben Sie Auskunft über Ihre Berufserfahrung. (Wo haben Sie gearbeitet? Wann?)
4. Beantworten Sie die Frage des Besitzers/der Besitzerin.
5. Sagen Sie, wann Sie anfangen können zu arbeiten.

© MEG Specimen Papers 1997/8

C Higher

You are staying in Germany and you see this advertisement in a local paper. You decide to telephone to offer your help. You will begin the conversation.

- **Grund des Anrufs**
- **Persönliche Angaben**
- **Bisherige praktische Erfahrung**

> **JUGENDKLUB**
> ◆◆◆◆**STAR**◆◆◆◆
>
> *Heidelbergerstr. 23*
>
> *Sind Sie sportlich?*
> *Sind Sie musikalisch?*
> *Kommen Sie gut mit Kindern aus?*
>
> Wir brauchen junge Leute, die in unserem Jugendklub aushelfen können.
>
> Weitere Informationen erhalten Sie
> von B. Krüger - Tel. 33 44 68

© London Examinations, a division of Edexcel Foundation 1996

(Solutions: pages 139–140)

Conversation

A Foundation

1. Was für einen Beruf haben deine Eltern?
2. Wie kommen deine Eltern zur Arbeit?
3. Hast du einen Job am Wochenende?
4. Was möchtest du nach der Schule machen?

B Higher

1. Was mußt du machen, um dein Geld zu verdienen?
2. Möchtest du Lehrer oder Lehrerin werden? Warum?
3. Was hast du als Betriebspraktikum gemacht?
4. Was sind die Vor- und Nachteile von dieser Arbeit?

(Solutions: page 141)

Speaking
Area E

E The **international world**

1 Life in other countries and communities

Rôle-play

Foundation/Higher

- Give yourself two minutes to prepare for this rôle-play. Then look at the model and listen to it on the cassette. To learn your responses you could follow the steps on page 80.

GELDWECHSELN

You are at an exchange bureau and you want to change £20 cash into Austrian Schillings. You would like some 5 Schilling coins.

1 Beantworten Sie die Frage von dem Angestellten.

2 Beantworten Sie die Frage von dem Angestellten.

3 Sie wollen

4 Nehmen Sie, was der Angestellte Ihnen anbietet, und bedanken Sie sich.

(Solution: page 142)

Conversation

Higher

- Look at the conversation on page 98. When you think you have learned the answers, cover them up and try to answer the questions. Then check your answers.

- You can also listen to the questions on the cassette, pause the machine and say your answers before playing the recording.

- The model answers may not be true for you. In preparing for your exam you can make a choice. You can change these answers to describe your breakfast and favourite meal. Or you can learn the answers above and use them. In your exam you should say the things which you are confident will get you good marks.

Speaking
Area E

Questions	Model answers
1 Um wieviel Uhr gibt es Frühstück? (A chance here to express an opinion.)	Bei uns frühstücken wir gegen Viertel vor acht. Es ist mein Lieblingsessen.
2 Und was ißt du normalerweise? (You can refer here to *normalerweise* and to *heute morgen*.)	Normalerweise esse ich Corn Flakes mit Milch und Zucker, ein Toastbrot mit Marmelade, und ich trinke Orangensaft dazu. Heute hatten wir keinen Orangensaft mehr, und so habe ich eine Tasse Tee getrunken.
3 Hast du ein Lieblingsgericht? (A chance here to express an opinion.)	Ja, ich esse sehr gern Rindfleisch mit Bratkartoffeln und Yorkshire Pudding. Das schmeckt wunderschön!
4 Was ist „Yorkshire Pudding"? Kannst du das erklären? (Explain fully: what it is, when you eat it, and how you make it.)	Das ist ein typisch englisches Gericht. Es ist ein bißchen wie ein Pfannkuchen. Man ißt das mit Rindfleisch. Es besteht aus Mehl, Eiern, Milch, Salz und Pfeffer. Man backt Yorkshire Pudding im Herd.
5 Hast du schon mal Sauerkraut gegessen? (A chance here to refer to past, present and future and to express an opinion.)	Nein, ich habe noch nie Sauerkraut gegessen, aber ich möchte es kosten. Das deutsche Essen gefällt mir sehr gut, und ich hoffe, immer etwas Neues bei meinen deutschen Freunden zu essen.

2 Tourism

Rôle-play

A Higher

> Give yourself four minutes to look at and prepare this Higher tier rôle-play. You need to work out what places in Germany you want to visit, where you want to stay and what kinds of activities you want to take part in. You also need to be ready to respond to any unexpected questions your teacher may be instructed to ask you.

You are in a tourist office in Austria and want to visit Germany next week. The Examiner will begin the conversation.

VERKEHRSAMT 🛈

RESTAURANTS

HOTELS

AUSFLÜGE

TÄGLICH 9.00–18.00 UHR

- **Wo und wann?**
- **Unterkunft**
- **Freizeitaktivitäten**

© London Examinations, a division of Edexcel Foundation 1996

(Solution: page 142)

Speaking
Area E

B Higher

- If you take the MEG exam, you will have to do a rôle-play like this, in the Higher tier. You can prepare it in advance and use a dictionary if you need to.

- You must also be ready to answer any questions and respond to any comments made by your teacher.

- Give yourself five minutes to prepare for this and try to include preparation for the questions and comments from your teacher. To get top marks you need to:
  1. talk about **all** the main points and to use your imagination to say more than the basic facts;
  2. avoid long pauses and speak confidently;
  3. refer to past, present and future;
  4. express and explain personal ideas or opinions.

The notes below give an outline of an exchange visit to Germany you made with your school. Tell the examiner what happened during the journey from England to Frankfurt. Be prepared to respond to any questions or comments from the examiner.

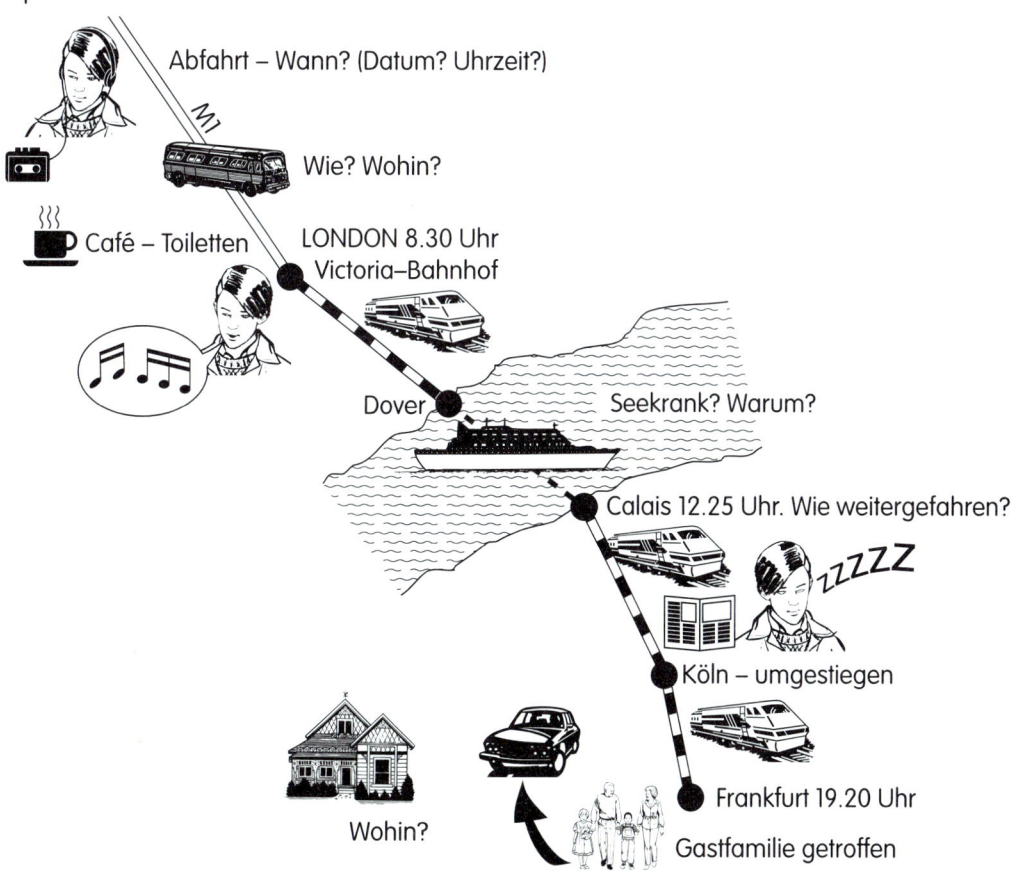

Abfahrt – Wann? (Datum? Uhrzeit?)

Wie? Wohin?

Café – Toiletten

LONDON 8.30 Uhr Victoria–Bahnhof

Dover

Seekrank? Warum?

Calais 12.25 Uhr. Wie weitergefahren?

Köln – umgestiegen

Wohin?

Frankfurt 19.20 Uhr
Gastfamilie getroffen

(Solution: page 143)

© MEG Specimen Papers 1997/8

Speaking
Area E

Conversation

Foundation and Foundation/Higher

> ◘ Examiners love to get you to talk about your holidays and this topic comes up often, so be prepared! Use the model below to learn the language you need to perform well.
>
> ◘ Work on these questions and answers along the lines suggested on page 80.

Questions

1. **Wo warst du neulich im Urlaub?**
   (A chance to refer to the past and to express an opinion.)

2. **Erzähl mir etwas von diesen Ferien.**
   (More references to the past and more opinions.)

3. **Hast du Ausflüge gemacht?**
   (You can refer to the past and the future here.)

4. **Was hast du zu Ostern gemacht?**
   (More references to the past and a justified opinion.)

5. **Wie findest du Ferien mit der Familie?**
   (Opinions and references to the future here.)

6. **Was für einen Ausflug würdest du für diese Gegend vorschlagen?**
   (Here you can refer to the present and express and explain an opinion.)

Model answers

Ich war mit meiner Familie an der Küste. Wir haben eine Woche auf einem Campingplatz verbracht. Es war toll!

Also, ich habe meistens am Strand Fußball gespielt und gebadet. Ja, und wir sind auch ins Kino gegangen. Das Wetter war echt super. Die Ferien waren prima!

Ja, wir haben einen schönen Tiergarten besucht. Die Löwen waren fantastisch, und die Affen sehr komisch. Ich möchte gern noch einmal dahin fahren.

Leider mußte ich diese Prüfung vorbereiten. Es war sehr langweilig, aber es mußte sein, weil dieses Examen so wichtig ist.

Ferien mit der Familie? Es geht, wenn man klein ist, aber dieses Jahr nach dem Examen fahre ich mit meinen Freunden in Urlaub. Das wird Spaß machen!

Es gibt nichts für Jugendliche hier in der Gegend, außer dem Meer, das nicht sehr weit entfernt ist. Ich würde einen Ausflug zur Küste vorschlagen. Da kann die ganze Familie Spaß haben!

3 Accommodation

Rôle-play

A Foundation

> ◘ Give yourself two minutes to prepare the rôle-play on page 101. Follow the steps on page 80 to learn the rôle-play, so that you'll be ready if something like it comes up in your exam.

Speaking
Area E

You are at a hotel in Germany and you want to book two rooms for your family for five nights. Your teacher will play the part of the hotel owner and will speak first.

Model answer

Lehrerin:		Wir sind in einem Hotel in Deutschland. Kann ich Ihnen helfen?
Du:		**Haben Sie Zimmer frei?**
Lehrerin:		Ja.
Du:		**Ich möchte ein Zimmer für zwei Personen und ein Einzelzimmer, bitte.**
Lehrerin:		Für wie lange?
Du:		**Für fünf Nächte, bitte.**
Lehrerin:		Ja, das geht.
Du:		**Was kostet das, bitte?**
Lehrerin:		DM 80 und DM 55.
Du:		**Danke schön.**

© Northern Examinations & Assessment Board 1996

B Foundation/Higher

- Use the technique you learnt earlier to prepare this rôle-play in two minutes. Note that:
  1. You are told what you need to book in the English introduction and you must decide on the number of rooms and beds.
  2. Think about what questions may be asked at the third point in the conversation and have some answers ready. Listen carefully to the unprepared question.
  3. Try to avoid using the same words as are in the instructions; you cannot get any marks for repeating them word for word.

- Don't look at the model answer on the next page and give your responses to the questions below. Then look at, listen to and learn the model answers. Work with a friend, if you can, and take turns to ask and answer the questions, without looking at the answers.

You are in a hotel in Austria and want to book rooms for your family. Your teacher will play the part of the receptionist and will speak first.

1. Begrüßen Sie die Empfangsdame.
2. Sagen Sie, was für Zimmer Sie wollen.
3. ! Beantworten Sie die Frage.
4. Fragen Sie nach dem Preis.
5. Fragen Sie, wann man essen kann.

Speaking
Area E

Model answers

Lehrerin: Sie sind mit Ihrer Familie in einem Hotel in Österreich. Sie möchten Zimmer buchen. Ich bin die Empfangsdame.

Guten Abend.

Du: **Guten Abend.**

Lehrerin: Was kann ich für Sie tun?

Du: **Ich möchte ein Doppelzimmer mit Bad und zwei Einzelzimmer mit Dusche, bitte.**

Lehrerin: Wie lange wollen Sie bleiben?

Du: **Drei Nächte, bitte. Bis zum fünften August.**

Lehrerin: In Ordnung.

Du: **Danke schön. Was kostet das?**

Lehrerin: ÖS 950 pro Nacht.

Du: **Gut. Um wieviel Uhr können wir essen, bitte?**

Lehrerin: Das Restaurant öffnet um halb sieben abends.

Du: **Vielen Dank.**

Key words and phrases

Haben Sie ein Zimmer frei?; Ich möchte ein Doppelzimmer/ein Einzelzimmer/mit Bad/mit Dusche; Für eine Nacht/für zwei Nächte; Bis zum fünften August; Was kostet das?; Um wieviel Uhr können wir essen, bitte?

C Higher

> Give yourself just two minutes to prepare this rôle-play. Try to anticipate what the receptionist will ask. The previous rôle-play should help with this. You should also expect some problems. Try to anticipate what these may be and prepare your responses. An important thing to remember with this sort of rôle-play is that it gives you a lot of power: you can take over the conversation from the beginning and say everything you have prepared.

You arrive at a hotel in Germany. It is quite late, you have no reservation and you have been travelling for a long time. You need a meal and somewhere to sleep. Your teacher will play the part of the receptionist and will start the conversation.

(Solution: page 144)

Speaking
Area E

4 The wider world

Conversation

> As usual you have the power to direct a conversation along the lines which suit you, so that you can say what you know you can say confidently and well. Once you have started to talk on a topic you have prepared for, keep talking. You don't have to wait for your teacher to ask you questions.

> Study this example. If you like it, learn it. If you don't, change it: write out what you want to say and ask your teacher to check your German. Then learn it and practise it.

Foundation/Higher

Model answers

1 Interessierst du dich für die Umwelt?
   Ja, ich interessiere mich sehr für Umweltprobleme. Es ist sehr wichtig, umweltfreundliche Produkte zu benutzen.

2 Und was machst du persönlich für die Umwelt?
   Zu Hause kaufen wir meistens Bioprodukte, zum Beispiel phosphatfreies Reinigungsmittel, recyceltes Papier und Getränke in Pfandflaschen.

3 Was ist das schlimmste Problem, deiner Meinung nach?
   Den Treibhauseffekt finde ich schrecklich. Die Erde erwärmt sich, weil man zu viele Autos hat und zu viele Spraydosen verwendet. Industrien verschmutzen die Luft, und die Bäume sterben.

4 Was sollte man für die Umwelt machen?
   Wir sollten öfter mit dem Rad fahren, oder mit dem Bus. Wir sollten auch weniger Plastikprodukte verwenden – Plastiktüten, Plastikflaschen und so weiter. Wir könnten auch viel mehr Bäume pflanzen.

5 Hast du schon einmal Deutschland oder Österreich besucht?
   Nein, aber ich lerne jetzt seit fünf Jahren Deutsch, und ich habe viel über Deutschland gelernt.

6 Was hast du über Deutschland gelernt?
   Also, Deutschland ist sehr schön mit vielen Wäldern und Bergen. Der Schwarzwald ist sehr bekannt – es gibt Schwarzwälderkirschtorte zum Beispiel, das ist sehr lecker! Deutschland hat viele sehr große Städte, zum Beispiel Frankfurt, Hamburg und Berlin, die Hauptstadt natürlich. Ich möchte sehr gern Berlin besuchen, weil es viele historische Sehenswürdigkeiten gibt, und auch, weil ich eine Brieffreundin in Berlin habe.

Or, if you have visited Germany, you could answer the two last questions like this:

Ja, ich bin mit der Schule nach Deutschland gefahren. Es war ein Schüleraustausch und ich war zwei Wochen bei einer deutschen Familie.

Wir haben viele tolle Ausflüge gemacht, zum Tiergarten, zum Themenpark, zum Wellenbad und auch nach Münster. Das ist eine schöne Stadt, die Altstadt und Fußgängerzone sind sehr malerisch.

Das Familienleben war sehr interessant – meine Familie war deutsch, aber meine Freundin war bei einer türkischen Familie. Sie hatte zuerst ein bißchen Heimweh, aber sie waren sehr freundlich und großzügig. Das Problem war die Sprache, weil die Mutter kaum ein Wort Deutsch sprechen konnte. Deutschland hat Einwohner aus vielen verschiedenen Ländern, und das macht es noch interessanter, finde ich. Man kann viel lernen.

Presentation
Foundation and Higher

- Some exam boards require you to give a short presentation at the start of your conversation. This is on a topic which you choose, and you can prepare in advance exactly what to say.

- You should talk for about two to three minutes and expect your teacher to discuss your presentation briefly with you when you have finished. You can use pictures or photos to illustrate what you say.

- Find out if you will have to do this. If you do, you could choose holidays as your topic and base your presentation on this model. This will help you get your conversation off to a really confident start.

- These questions will help you to prepare a good presentation:
    1. Wohin bist du gefahren?
    2. Wie bist du gefahren? Mit dem Zug?
    3. Mit wem warst du dort?
    4. Wann war das?
    5. Wo hast du gewohnt?
    6. Was hast du gemacht?
    7. Was hast du gesehen?
    8. Wie war das Wetter?
    9. Möchtest du wieder dahin fahren?

- One thing you could do is to present orally something you have learnt to write. See, for example, page 101 of *Revise for GCSE German Reading and Writing*. Or you could prepare something new, using the questions above to guide you. This could produce a presentation like the one on the right.

- If you decide to base your presentation on this model, add some ideas of your own and ask your teacher to check that your German is correct. Then learn it by heart. Get to the point where you can cover it up and use only the questions and pictures on the left to remind you of what you want to say. Listen to the recording many times and when you feel ready, stop the tape from time to time and try to say from memory what comes next. Carry on for as long as you can.

- In your exam you can use pictures to help remind you what to say and a few written notes. So, for your presentation you could put your questions and pictures onto small cards.

Speaking
Presentation

Introduction

Ich möchte von meinen Ferien sprechen. Es war wirklich toll – ich werde diese Ferien nie vergessen. Ich habe hier einige Fotos, die ich geknipst habe.

1 Wohin bist du gefahren?

2 Wie bist du gefahren? Mit dem Zug?

Mein Vater hatte drei Wochen Urlaub, und wir sind mit dem Auto und dem Wohnwagen nach Österreich gefahren. Die Fahrt war ziemlich lang, aber wir haben zweimal unterwegs übernachtet, einmal in Frankreich und dann in der Schweiz.

3 Mit wem warst du dort?

4 Wann war das?

Meine Schwester, Julia, und mein Bruder, James, waren auch mit mir und meinen Eltern. Es war letzten Sommer im August.

5 Wo hast du gewohnt?

Am dritten Tag sind wir auf dem Campingplatz in der Nähe von Salzburg angekommen. Es war herrlich – ein kleiner Fluß, schöne Wälder und viel Platz für unseren Wohnwagen.

6 Was hast du gemacht?

7 Was hast du gesehen?

Wir haben Salzburg besichtigt. Das ist eine tolle Stadt, wo viel los ist. Die Geschäfte haben meiner Mutter und meiner Schwester gut gefallen. Mein Bruder und ich haben das italienische Eis sehr lecker gefunden. Wir haben auch im Fluß gebadet und sind jeden Tag im Wald gewandert.

8 Wie war das Wetter?

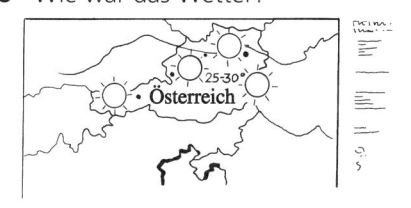

Das Wetter war wirklich schön. Wir hatten jeden Tag Sonnenschein und Temperaturen von 25 bis 30 Grad. Wir sind alle schön braun geworden.

9 Möchtest du wieder dahin fahren?

Diese Ferien haben der ganzen Familie so gut gefallen, daß wir nächstes Jahr auch auf den selben Campingplatz fahren wollen. Das finde ich toll, weil Österreich ein besonders schönes Land ist. Leider ist alles ein bißchen teuer, und ich muß einen Job finden, um Geld für das nächste Mal zu sparen.

Solutions: Listening

Part 1

1
A *Sport*; **B** *Sport*; **C** *Kunst*; **D** *Musik* [4]

2
1 b, c, e, f [4]
2 *Bonbons* or *Kaugummi* [1]
3 *40 DM* [1]

3
1 A; **2** B; **3** A [3]

4
a A; b A; c A [3]

5
1 H; **2** C; **3** C; **4** C; **5** C; **6** C;
7 H; **8** H; **9** H; **10** H; **11** S; **12** C [12]

6
a *Anja Petersen*; 17; *Dornbirn* [3]
b *Keine (Geschwister)*; *Handball, Kino*; *Hund* [4]

7
A [1]

8
a *Abenteuerfilm* or *für Kinder*
b *Samstag*
c *17.00* or *fünf Uhr* [3]

9
1 B, D, E, C, G [5]
2 C [1]
3 a *Fernsehen* [1]
   b *Judo* [2]
   c *Volleyball* [1]
4 a *Samstag*
   b *Freitag*
   c *Sonntag* [3]
5 a *Wandern*
   b *Schwimmen*
   c *Fußball(spiel)* [3]

10
Ein paar Wörter
1 E; 2 F; 3 A; 4 C; 5 B; 6 D [6]

1 *Peter, du sollst Anna um 4 Uhr im Café treffen.* [2]

2 a 19.15
    b DM 15
    c DM 11 [3]
3 a Play tennis
    b Grandmother visiting
    c 2.30 [3]

11
Richtig: a, b, e
Falsch: c, d, f, g [7]

12
Ein paar Wörter
1 C; 2 E; 3 I; 4 B; 5 G;
6 A; 7 I; 8 D; 9 F; 10 H

1 A [1]
2 A [1]

13
1 B [1]
2 4 [1]
3 a 1
   b 300 g
   c 2 kg
   d 250 g [4]

14
1 C = 15 [1]
2 B = 8 Uhr [1]
3 A = *Gleis 5* [1]
4 DM 2,50 [1]
5 a *in 3$\frac{1}{2}$ Stunden*
   b *noch nicht fertig*
   c *zu teuer*
   d *mit dem Bus* [4]

15
1 G
2 E
3 B
4 D [4]

16
1 A, C, F, H, L, M, P, S [8]
2 a A [1]
   b A [1]
   c B [1]

17
1. Headache tablets/aspirin
2. Using a mobile phone/phoning between 20.00 and 7.00
3. A new type of pizza
4. A toothbrush [4]

18
a. 0261
b. 3 31 34
c. 2 41 21
d. 2 96 40
e. 3 50 50
f. 12 55 70 [6]

19
a. DM 2,99
b. DM 0,80
c. DM 17,60
d. DM 5,25 [4]

20
a. *März*
b. *Regen/regnen*
c. *Zug*
d. *acht Uhr*
e. *(vor der) Schule*
f. i) *Rathaus* ii) *Museum*
g. *Rad*
h. *Wanderung* [9]

21
a. A D B E F [5]
b. B C A D [4]

22
Ein paar Wörter
1 C; 2 G; 3 E; 4 A; 5 H; 6 J; 7 B; 8 I; 9 F; 10 D

a. Italy – by bus/visit Rome [2]
b. Austria – mountains/hike/ride bikes/skiing/resting [2]
c. France – sand and sea/swim/laze about/lie in the sun [2]

Part 2

1
1.
 a. Brigitte
 b. Dieter
 c. Inge [3]

2.
 d. Brigitte
 e. Brigitte [2]

2
c, d, e, g, h, j, k, l, n [9]

3
Ein paar Zahlen
1 D; 2 E; 3 A; 4 C; 5 B; 6 H; 7 I; 8 F; 9 J; 10 G

a. 29
b. *Frankreich*
c. *Go-kart fahren/Laufen/Rockmusik*
d. 1983 [4]

4
Ein paar Zahlen
1 B; 2 E; 3 F; 4 A; 5 C; 6 D

A *Sven*
B *Lotte*
C *Jan*
D *Anna* [4]

5
At station/8 o'clock/meet/8.30/outside station/phone if not possible/before 7 o'clock. [7]

6
a. bus
b. Number 4
c. swimming pool
d. church
e. opposite (the church)
f. 661352 [6]

7
1 E; **2** C; **3** B; **4** F [4]

8
A DM 6,99
B *Apfelsinen*
C *Computer*
D *Sportschuhe*
E DM 75 [5]

Solutions
Listening

9

Name	Geschenk	Weitere Informationen
a Herr Müller	Buch über Fußball (1)	Geschichte – Ursprünge (1) (des englischen Fußballspiels) (1)
b Frau Meyer	CD (1)	liebt klassische Musik (1) – CD von einem englischen Komponisten (1)
c Herr Krause	Kochbuch (1)	kocht gern (1) – englische Rezepte (1)
d Frau Decker	Teekanne (1)	trinkt sehr gern Tee (1) – aus England (1)

[12]

10
Richtig: 2 [1]
Falsch: 1, 3 [2]

11
A 1; B 3; C 4; D 6; E 5; F 2 [6]

12
Richtig: a, b, c, e
Falsch: d [5]

13
a *Autowerkstatt/Garage*
b *Autos reparieren/Autos waschen*
c *7.30–16.00* [3]

14
1 B; 2 E; 3 A (example); 4 G; 5 D; 6 F; 7 C (example) [5]

15
Richtig: b, d, f [3]
Falsch: a, c, e [3]

16
1 A, B, D [3]
2 C [1]
3 A, F [2]
4 A, E [2]
5 B, D [2]
6 A [2]

17
Richtig: d [1]
Falsch: a, b, c [3]

Part 3

1
a *Schlechte Lehrer – schreien, wenn man nichts falsch macht. Einige coole Lehrer.* [1]
b *Locker – Schüler wählen die Themen, die sie lernen wollen. Macht Spaß.* [1]
c *Schlimm – Schüler machen, was sie wollen.* [1]
d *Die schlimmste Klasse an der ganzen Schule.* [1]
e *Der Lehrer ist sehr gelassen. Sie machen nicht mehr richtig Englisch.* [1]
f *Kompliziert. Lehrer erklären schlecht. „Die Vergangenheit". Lehrer reden manchmal deutsch, manchmal englisch.* [1]

2
a *10/(oder) 11*
b *Unsinn*
c *nicht gut*
d *gut/wie die Kings*
e *Schulfreundin*
f *13*
g *erwachsen/attraktiv*
h *er hat sie gekauft/von niemanden*
i *14*
j *fitter*
k *joggen*
l *riechen*
m *schmecken* [13]

3
a *illegal; gefährlich* [2]
b *sie langweilen sich; es macht Spaß; Streß in der Schule* [3]
c *schwach* [1]

Solutions
Listening

4
a schlecht/nicht gut/weich/ohne Geschmack
b Schwarzbrot/Roggenbrot
c 14/viele/mehr
d (deutsche) Brötchen
e das Gemüse
f Heinz
g zu viel
h nicht (zu) stark gekocht/gut gekocht
i 3 Wochen
j Vegetarier
k zu viel Fett
l hat einen Bauernhof/ist Bauer/züchtet Schweine
m Kinder [13]

5
a change money [1]
b sunglasses and red moustache [2]

6
a Anna
b Peter
c Peter
d Anna [4]

7
a gestern abend [1]
b großartig [1]
c die Stimmen sind furchtbar/man versteht kein Wort davon [2]
d keine richtige Musik/die Sänger schreien/das kann man nicht Musik nennen. [2]
e Gruppen bringen tolle Sachen/richtige Texte kommen vor/sie haben etwas übers Leben zu sagen/sie haben etwas über die Umwelt zu sagen. [3]
f Die Texte sind O.K. [1]
g i) Die Opern werden immer noch aufgeführt. [1]
   ii) Die Popmusik wird vergessen sein. [1]
h Sie haben keine Kultur/Sie sind für Kultur nicht offen. [1]

8
1 a Theater; [1]
  b Der Gast würde nicht (alles) verstehen. [1]
2 a Rockkonzert; [1]
  b Nicht für die ältere Generation – es soll ein Familienausflug sein. [1]
3 a Bootsausflug; [1]
  b Es ist ein bißchen teuer. [1]
4 großzügig/unternehmungslustig [2]

9
1 C; 2 D (or C); 3 A; 4 F; [4]

10
1 Richtig: a, d, g, j
  Falsch: b, c, e, f, h, i, k, l [12]
2 a Boris [1]
  b Anna [1]
  c Boris [1]
  d Anna [1]
3 a Er wohnt auf dem Land/Sein [2]
    Freund wohnt in der Stadt. [1]
  b mit dem Fahrrad [1]
  c Er geht zur Bushaltestelle/ (Er fährt) mit dem Bus. [1]
  d (die) Infrastruktur
    Straßenbahn
    (viel) mehr Angebote [3]
  e Tanzkurs [1]
  f Man muß mit dem Fahrrad fahren; Man bleibt zu Hause. [2]
  g Man geht nicht in die Stadt/ Die Eltern bringen einen dahin. [2]

11
1 a Es ist ihr egal. [1]
  b was ihr gefällt/sportliche Sachen [2]
  c von ihrer Schwester/vom Markt [2]
2 200 g Mehl, 200 g Butter, 2 Eier, eine Zitrone, 100 g Zucker [5]
3 a B [1]
  b Sein Gürtel ist sehr alt./Er guckte sich die neuen Gürtel im Kaufhaus an. [1]
  c Handschuhe – zu teuer; Armbanduhr – er hat die alte Armbanduhr von seinem Vater./Seine alte Armbanduhr gefällt ihm gut. [2]

Solutions
Listening

12
1. **A** You quickly get used to driving on the left. [1]
   B b; Goes to distant villages/cheaper [2]
2. a One woman dead; four seriously injured [1]
   b Car crashed into tanker, tanker crashed into second car [1]
   c Closed the motorway for four hours. [1]

13
1. a *13. Klasse* [1]
   b *Abitur* [1]
   c *19* [1]
   d *französische Familie* [1]
   e *Frankreich* [1]
   f *ein Jahr* [1]
   g *Englisch* [1]
   h *Englisch-Französisch* [1]
   i *Fremdsprachenlehrerin* [2]
   j *5 Jahre* [1]
   k *(in) England* [1]
2. a *Krankenschwester* [1]
   b *Fahrlehrer - mit guten Qualifikationen* [1]
3. Monika a *(im) Altersheim*
           b *2 Wochen*
           c *3 Stunden*

   Georg a *gut/eine gute Erfahrung*
          b *(in der) Küche*
          c *Die Leute waren freundlich*

   Markus a *schrecklich/nicht gut*
          b *um 6.30 Uhr*
          c *im Supermarkt arbeiten* [9]
4. a Start 1 hour earlier. [1]
   b German – goes home earlier in afternoon. [2]
   c Advantages – nice, helpful colleagues. Disadvantages – the journey to work is long/the work is not interesting. [2]
   d Start computer training [1]
5. a *Arbeit – 54 Stunden in der Woche*
      Ferien – 6–8 Tage Urlaub
      Geld – wenig Lohn (250–300 Mark)
      Lebensstandard – kein Auto/Motorrad, Margarine, nicht Butter
      Familie – wichtiger/stärker [5]
   b *Geld – viel/mehr Geld*
      Lebensstandard – Auto und Fernseher, Butter
      Familie – nicht so stark/wichtig [5]

14
1. B [1]
2. A [1]
3. D [1]
4. C [1]
5. A [1]
6. A [1]
7. A, C, D [2]
8. *Auto bestätigen/(andere) Freizeitwünsche/(besondere) Eßwünsche* [3]

15
a *(nach) Südfrankreich* [1]
b *Strand und Meer genießen* [2]

16
1. C [1]
2. B [1]
3. D, B, A, C [4]

17
c, e, h [3]

18
Richtig: a, c, e, g, i
Falsch: b, d, f, h [9]

Listening transcript

Part 1

1
Also, morgen gehen wir in die Schule. Die erste Stunde ist Deutsch, und dann habe ich Englisch. Nach der ersten Pause habe ich eine Doppelstunde Sport. Hoffentlich werden wir Handball spielen. Nachher gibt es Kunst und die letzte Stunde ist Musik – furchtbar, der Musiklehrer ist immer schlecht gelaunt. Also, morgen mußt du früh aufstehen – die Schule beginnt schon um 8.00 Uhr.

2
– Was machst du zu Hause, um deinen Eltern zu helfen?
– Ich – gar nichts! Meine Mutter arbeitet nicht und macht gerne alles im Haus und im Garten.
– Du hast es aber gut! Ich muß viel machen, da Mutti und Vati arbeiten. Ich gehe jeden Tag einkaufen – das macht Spaß, ich kaufe mir gewöhnlich Bonbons oder Kaugummi. Aber spülen, den Tisch decken, mein Zimmer aufräumen, das ist alles sehr langweilig.
– Hoffentlich bekommst du Taschengeld dafür?
– Natürlich – 40 DM pro Woche.

3
– Was fehlt Ihnen?
– Ich habe Fieber und Kopfschmerzen.
– Seit wann haben Sie das?
– Seit drei Tagen. Der Kopf tut mir weh.
– Haben Sie Tabletten eingenommen?
– Nein.
– Ich werde Ihnen ein Rezept schreiben. Bringen Sie es zur Apotheke.

4
Beispiel: Eine Cola, bitte!

1 Ich möchte eine Tasse Kaffee, bitte.
2 Ich nehme ein Stück Kuchen, bitte.
3 Das macht fünf Mark zwanzig zusammen.

5
H – Ich bin hungrig. Ich habe heute nicht viel gegessen.
C – Hast du denn nicht gefrühstückt, Heinz?
H – Nein, ich bin zu spät aufgestanden. Und in der Pause habe ich nur ein Brot gegessen.
C – Ich habe heute Corn Flakes zum Frühstück gehabt und dann noch einen Apfel. In der Pause habe ich auch einen Apfel gegessen. Jetzt werde ich zu Mittag nur ein wenig Wurst und Käse essen und vielleicht Obst.
H – Wir essen zu Mittag immer sehr viel.
C – Meine Eltern sind zu Mittag nicht da, und ich muß mein eigenes Mittagessen machen. Eine richtige Mahlzeit gibt es dann am Abend.
H – Als ich in England war, habe ich immer viel gefrühstückt – Corn Flakes, Schinken mit Eiern, Toast, Orangenmarmelade, Tee…
C – Bei meiner englischen Gastfamilie hat es nur Orangensaft mit Toast gegeben. Steffi, du warst doch auch in England. Was hat es bei dir gegeben?
S – Ich mußte jeden Tag Müsli essen.
C – Naja, in unserem Englischlehrbuch ist immer vom großen englischen Frühstück die Rede, aber ich mußte nur mit Orangensaft und Tee auskommen. So ein Pech!

Ein paar Wörter (page 15)

1 Religion   Religion
2 Garage   Garage
3 Adresse   Adresse
4 Finger   Finger
5 Student   Student
6 Station   Station
7 England   England
8 Minute   Minute
9 Hand   Hand
10 Supermarkt   Supermarkt

6
a Grüß dich! Ich bin Anja, Anja Petersen. Das schreibt man A N J A P E T E R S E N. Ich bin 17 Jahre alt und wohne in Österreich in Dornbirn, D O R N B I R N.
b Ich habe keine Geschwister, aber viele Freunde! Was ich gern in meiner Freizeit mache? Also, ich spiele sehr gern Handball und gehe oft ins Kino. Ich habe einen Hund, weißt du? Einen großen Hund!

7
Ich bin 13 Jahre alt. Ich bin sehr groß und habe kurze lockige Haare. Ich habe ein ziemlich langes Gesicht, und ich trage gerne eine Sonnenbrille.

8
Hier ist der telefonische Anrufbeantworter des Capitol

Listening
Transcript

Kinos, Bad Tölz:
André – Der große Abenteuerfilm, Samstag um 17.00 Uhr.

9
1 Also, meine Hobbys: Ich gehe schwimmen und ich reite gern. Ich treffe mich mit Freunden. Ich fahre in Urlaub, wenn ich Zeit und Geld habe. Ich gehe zu Partys. Ab und zu koche ich auch ganz gerne, und ich lese.

2 – Was machst du mit deinem Taschengeld?
– Meistens kaufe ich Zeitschriften und Schallplatten.

3 Du wolltest mal wissen, was ich in meiner Freizeit mache? Also, ich bin Mitglied in einem Tischtennisverein. Jeden Freitag spiele ich Tischtennis in der Turnhalle. Manchmal spiele ich auch Volleyball … ja, Volleyball, das macht auch Spaß. Was ich nicht gerne mache? Also, ich sehe nicht gern fern … Fernsehen ist ziemlich langweilig. Na, ich gehe einmal in der Woche zum Judokurs. Judo ist echt toll. Abends sehe ich meistens fern, am liebsten sehe ich Krimis. In der Schule müssen wir meistens Volleyball spielen, und das gefällt mir gar nicht. Volleyball ist viel zu anstrengend, das macht gar keinen Spaß.

4 – Hallo, Jan. Was machst du am Wochenende?
– Am Freitag werde ich tanzen gehen, und dann am Samstag wahrscheinlich am Computer spielen und am Sonntag fernsehen.

5 – Und über's Wochenende? Ich würde gern wandern. Was meint ihr? Dieter?
– Oh nein, Ina, bitte nicht! Im Moment ist es viel zu kalt zum Wandern. Wollen wir vielleicht Schwimmen gehen? Das kostet auch nicht viel. Was meinst du dazu, Ulrike?
– Das will ich auch nicht! Ich möchte lieber zum Fußballspiel gehen – die Karten habe ich sowieso schon gekauft.

Ein paar Wörter *(page 19)*
1 Fußballspiel   Fußballspiel
2 treffen   treffen
3 am Computer spielen am Computer spielen
4 wandern   wandern
5 vier Uhr   vier Uhr
6 fernsehen   fernsehen

10
1 – Hallo, Anna hier. Ich möchte bitte Peter sprechen.
– Er ist nicht da. Kann ich ihm etwas ausrichten?
– Ja, bitte sehr. Können Sie ihm sagen, daß ich am Freitag nicht kommen kann. Oma ist krank und ich muß sie besuchen. Wir können uns aber am Samstag treffen.
– Wann denn?
– Sagen wir mal um 4 Uhr im Café.
– O.K., in Ordnung, das sage ich ihm.

2 Guten Tag. Vielen Dank für den Anruf. Für Auskünfte über unsere heutigen Vorstellungen hören Sie bitte weiter. Für andere Auskünfte rufen Sie bitte ab 16 Uhr die Nummer 50 38 07 an. Heute läuft im Saal 1 „Dracula" um 19.30 Uhr und 22.00 Uhr. Im Saal 2 haben Sie „Forrest Gump" um 16.45 Uhr und 19.15 Uhr. Eintrittspreise – Erwachsene – DM 15, Kinder (5 bis 13 Jahre) – DM 10, Ermäßigung für Studenten, Rentner und Arbeitslosen – DM 11. Vielen Dank!

3 – Hallo Dieter. Was machst du?
– Grüß dich, Bruno. Tja, nichts Besonderes.
– Wollen wir heute nachmittag Tennis spielen?
– Nein, tut mir leid. Meine Oma kommt zu Besuch.
– Schade. Wie wär's mit Dienstagnachmittag?
– Gut – um halb drei vor dem Park. Tschüs!
– Bis dann!

11
– Kappeldorf ist eine alte Stadt, sie hat jetzt ihre 900-Jahr-Feier. Sie hat ein sehr schönes Schloß … und es gibt einen schönen Wald in der Nähe.
– Also, du wohnst sehr gern in Kappeldorf?
– Ja, aber leider ist Kappeldorf so klein, daß es kein Kino hat. Auch mit dem Einkaufen ist es schlecht. Es gibt nur ein paar Geschäfte, wo man Lebensmittel kaufen kann.
– Wo kaufst du denn Kleider?
– Da muß ich nach Osnabrück fahren.
– Wie kommst du dahin? Mit der Straßenbahn?
– Nein, meine Eltern bringen mich dahin.

Ein paar Wörter *(page 21)*
1 geradeaus   geradeaus
2 bis zur Ampel   bis zur Ampel
3 an der Post vorbei an der Post vorbei
4 rechts   rechts
5 über die Brücke   über die Brücke
6 links   links
7 zu Fuß   zu Fuß
8 gegenüber   gegenüber
9 an der Kreuzung   an der Kreuzung
10 um die Ecke   um die Ecke

12
Beispiel: – Entschuldigen Sie bitte, wo ist die Post?
– Nehmen Sie die erste Straße rechts.

1 – Entschuldigen Sie bitte, wo ist das Kaufhaus?
– Gehen Sie geradeaus, und nehmen Sie die zweite Straße links.

2 Das ist nicht weit. Fahren Sie geradeaus, und biegen Sie an der zweiten Kreuzung links ab. Das Parkhaus ist auf der rechten Seite.

13
1 Also, was brauch' ich heute? Ich brauche noch ein Kilo Zucker und ein halbes Pfund Kaffee.

2 Bücher gibt es im zweiten Stock und Damenkleidung im ersten Stock. Sportartikel gibt es ganz oben im vierten Stock.

3 Ja, man braucht:
200 g Mehl
1 Ei
300 g Butter
2 Kilo Äpfel
250 g Zucker

14
1 Fahren Sie mit der Linie fünfzehn. Sie fährt alle fünf Minuten direkt dorthin.

2 Der nächste Bus kommt um acht Uhr.

3 Der nächste Zug nach Hamburg fährt von Gleis fünf ab.

4 Eine Einzelkarte kostet zwei Mark fünfzig.

5 – Entschuldigen Sie, ich will zum Flughafen.
– Wann müssen Sie denn dort sein?
– Mein Flug geht in dreieinhalb Stunden.
– Na, dann müssen Sie sich aber beeilen.
– Wieso?
– Der neue Flughafen ist bei Erding. Das ist ungefähr 35 Kilometer von München entfernt.
– Oh nein!
– Oh doch!
– Dann muß ich jetzt so schnell wie möglich eine S- oder U-Bahn zu diesem Flughafen finden.
– Tja, eine S- oder U-Bahnverbindung zum Flughafen, das gibt es nicht. Jetzt ist der neue Flughafen da, doch die Bahn ist noch nicht fertig.
– Ja, wie komm' ich dann zu diesem blöden Flughafen?
– Entweder nehmen Sie ein Taxi ...
– Kommt gar nicht in Frage. So viel Geld hab' ich nun doch nicht. Wo ist die Bushaltestelle für Erding?
– Am Hauptbahnhof.

15
– Ich bin Katja, und bin 18 Jahre alt. Ich habe die Schule verlassen und mache eine Ausbildung als Köchin in einem großen Hotel.

– Ich heiße Jens und bin 16 Jahre alt. Ich mag Tiere besonders gern und Wandern auch. Ich wohne auf dem Land. Mein Vater ist Bauer, aber ich möchte gerne Tierarzt werden.

– Ich heiße Jörg. Sport ist mein Leben – ich muß unbedingt das Abitur schaffen, um ein Studium als Sportlehrer zu machen. Mein Lieblingssport ist Handball.

– Mein Name ist Bärbel. Meine Mutter ist Sekretärin – sie findet ihre Arbeit sehr langweilig. So was würde mir nicht gefallen. Ich will auf die Universität gehen, um Architektur zu studieren.

– Ich heiße Peter und bin 15 Jahre alt. Ich gehe nicht gern in die Schule und möchte nächstes Jahr eine Ausbildung als Elektriker anfangen. Meine Eltern sind ganz zufrieden damit.

16
1 – Guten Morgen, Herr Clarke. Haben Sie eine gute Reise gehabt?
– Ja, danke schön.
– Woher kommen Sie?
– Aus Warrington, in England. Das ist in der Nähe von Liverpool.
– Ist Warrington eine große Stadt?
– Nein, nicht besonders groß. Liverpool ist größer.
– Spielen Sie Fußball?
– Ja, aber ich spiele lieber Cricket.
– Haben Sie noch andere Interessen?
– Ja, ich lese gern und gehe oft ins Kino. Ich habe auch einen Samstagsjob.
– Was machen Sie in Ihrem Samstagsjob?
– Ich arbeite in einem Restaurant. Ich helfe in der Küche. Ich spüle Besteck und Geschirr, und ich helfe beim Gemüseschälen.
– Was für eine Schule besuchen Sie?
– Ich besuche eine Gesamtschule für Jungen und Mädchen von 11 bis 18 Jahren.
– Was sind Ihre Lieblingsfächer?
– Deutsch und Geographie.
– Seit wann lernen Sie Deutsch?
– Seit sieben Jahren.
– Lernen Sie auch andere Fremdsprachen?
– Ja, ich habe auch Französisch gelernt, aber jetzt nicht mehr.
– Warum wollen Sie in Deutschland arbeiten?
– Um mein Deutsch zu verbessern.

2 a Meine Eltern sind beide berufstätig. Mein Vater ist Lehrer.

Listening
Transcript

    b Meine Mutter arbeitet auch. Sie ist Ärztin.
    c Ich interessiere mich für Informatik, und ich möchte mit Computern arbeiten.

17
- Es gibt Momente, da kann man Kopfschmerzen wirklich nicht gebrauchen – Aspirin ist immer für dich da!
- Nur 29 Pf. – zwischen 20 und 7 Uhr. So preiswert kann eine Minute mobil telefonieren sein!
- Die neue Pizza Napoli ist noch größer und schmeckt wie beim Italiener!
- Die neue Phillips – eine Zahnbürste, die alles richtig macht!

18
Hier spricht Trudi vom Büro Schmidt in Koblenz. Hier sind die Telefonnummern, die Sie brauchen. Alle Büros sind in Koblenz. Die Vorwahl ist also jedesmal 0261. Freibad Oberwerth: 2 96 40. Verkehrsbüro: 3 31 34. Firma Bock: 12 55 70. Hotel Panorama: 3 50 50. Privatnummer von Herrn Schmidt: 2 41 21.

19
Guten Morgen, meine Damen und Herren. Heute haben Sie Glück! Es gibt viele Sonderangebote bei Kaufpark ... Ein Kilo italienische Tomaten ... nur DM 2,99. Deutsche Schokolade ... 80 Pf. Wenn Sie Durst haben, kaufen Sie Birkhofs Bier ... 20 Flaschen ... DM 17,60. Als leckeren Nachtisch gibt es Mövenpick Eiscreme ... DM 5,25. Kaufen Sie frisch, freundlich und preiswert bei Kaufpark!

20
Unsere Partnerschule wollte, daß wir im November kommen. Wir wollten aber im März nach Deutschland fahren, und das haben sie akzeptiert. Einen Mantel sollte jeder Schüler einpacken, denn es kann viel regnen. Wir werden mit dem Zug über Brüssel fahren und in Köln umsteigen. Wir machen einen Ausflug nach Hannover. Wir treffen uns um acht Uhr vor der Schule. In Hannover besichtigen wir das alte Rathaus in der Stadtmitte und ein Museum für Heimatkunde am Stadtrand. Leider gibt es keinen Linienbus. Also fahren wir jeden Tag mit dem Rad zur Schule. Dieses Jahr wollen wir am letzten Abend eine Wanderung durch den Wald machen.

21
Hier in Koblenz gibt es drei Campingplätze. Camping Grünwald hat einen Supermarkt und ein Café. Der Campingplatz Hofbauer ist größer. Es gibt da natürlich Toiletten und Duschen, und ein Lebensmittelgeschäft, verstehst du, einen kleinen Supermarkt. Für Kinder gibt es ein schönes beheiztes Freibad. Man kann auch Fahrräder mieten. Es ist wirklich nicht teuer, ein Fahrrad für eine Woche zu mieten. Da können die Kinder schwimmen und Radfahren. Echt toll! Der andere Campingplatz, Camping Mosel, ist kleiner. Er hat ein kleines Geschäft und ein Café, aber keine anderen Einrichtungen außer Toiletten und Duschen.

Ein paar Wörter *(page 28)*
1 Irland   Irland
2 Afrika   Afrika
3 Italien   Italien
4 Schottland Schottland
5 USA   USA
6 Belgien   Belgien
7 Amerikaner Amerikaner
8 Dänemark   Dänemark
9 England   England
10 Spanisch   Spanisch

22
- Machen Sie eine Busreise durch Italien. Besuchen Sie die Sehenswürdigkeiten der Hauptstadt Rom.
- Fahren Sie nach Österreich in die Berge – Wandern – Radfahren – Skifahren, oder sich einfach ausruhen.
- Fahr im Urlaub nach Frankreich – genieße Strand und Meer – Schwimmen – Faulenzen, oder in der Sonne liegen!

Part 2

1
1
- Ach, Dieter, das war wieder eine langweilige Stunde. Ich kann Mathe einfach nicht ausstehen.
- Na ja, Brigitte, das kommt wahrscheinlich daher, daß du in dem letzten Test wieder eine schlechte Note hattest.
- Das ist aber nicht der Grund. Was meinst du, Inge?
- Ach, Dieter, du mußt doch zugeben, der Lehrer ist auch nicht besonders gut.
- Nun, Inge, du machst Mathematik und Naturwissenschaften nicht gerade gern.
- Ja, ja, ich weiß, die Fächer machen dir ja Spaß, Dieter. In Kunst und Sport bin ich aber viel besser.

2
- Was machst du eigentlich gern, Brigitte?
- Meine Lieblingsfächer sind Englisch und Französisch. Für meine Aufsätze bekomme ich regelmäßig eine Eins. Das kann ich einfach. Und du, Inge?
- Also, Brigitte, Sprachen kann ich überhaupt nicht, das weißt du schon. Für die meisten Fächer muß ich ganz schön viel machen. Und da kommen die vielen Hausaufgaben noch

dazu. Und das dauert jeden Tag mindestens vier Stunden. Die Lehrer glauben, wir haben nichts anderes zu tun.
– Komm, Inge! In zwei Wochen sind Ferien, und dann kannst du dich wieder erholen. Ich freue mich schon darauf.
– Warum denkt ihr immer nur an Ferien? Die finde ich sterbenslangweilig.

2
– Nikki schläft nicht gerne zu lange – nicht einmal jetzt in den Sommerferien. Sie steht sofort auf. Wenn das elfjährige Mädchen morgens aufsteht, ist sie allein mit ihrem kleinen Vogel, einem Wellensittich, in ihrem Schlafzimmer. Die Eltern haben beide einen Job und sind schon im Büro. Also macht sich Nikki selbst ihr Frühstück.
– Morgens, wenn ich aufwache, bin ich alleine, dann frühstücke ich, im Garten, wenn es schön ist, dann telefoniere ich mit Daniela, meiner besten Freundin aus der Schule. Dann gehen wir vielleicht am Nachmittag zusammen zum Fluß hinunter.

Ein paar Zahlen (page 30)
1	140	140
2	1932	1932
3	49	49
4	1875	1875
5	1200	1200
6	2500	2500
7	1789	1789
8	458	458
9	1981	1981
10	1944	1944

3
Ein Interview mit Michael Schumacher
– Darf ich jetzt ein paar persönliche Fragen stellen?
– Ja, sicher.
– Wie alt sind Sie?
– Ich bin 29.
– Wohnen Sie hier in Deutschland?
– Nein, ich wohne in Frankreich.
– Was sind Ihre Hobbys?
– Natürlich Go-Kart-Fahren, Laufen, Rockmusik.
– Wie alt waren Sie, als Sie mit dem Autorennen angefangen haben?
– Ich habe mit vier Jahren das Go-Kart-Fahren angefangen. Mein erstes Rennen war 1983.

Ein paar Wörter (page 31)
1 Was liest du?
2 ein englisches Buch
3 ein ganz tolles Buch
4 über Pferde
5 die Umwelt
6 zur Zeit

4
– Was liest du im Moment, Jan?
– Ich lese zur Zeit ein englisches Buch – ich muß mich wirklich anstrengen!
– Was liest du, Anna?
– Im Moment lese ich Krimis.
– Was liest du, Sven?
– Ich lese ein Buch über die Umwelt.
– Was liest du, Lotte?
– Ich lese Tierbücher sehr gern. Ich lese ein ganz tolles Buch über Pferde in Frankreich.

5
Also, kannst du bitte John sagen, daß ich erst um acht Uhr am Bahnhof bin? Hast du verstanden, um acht Uhr am Bahnhof, ja? Ich treffe ihn also um halb neun vor dem Bahnhof … halb neun … vor dem Bahnhof. Wenn er mich heute abend um halb neun nicht treffen kann, soll er mich anrufen, um Bescheid zu sagen, aber er muß vor sieben anrufen. Ist das klar? Er soll mich vor sieben anrufen, wenn es mit dem Treffen um halb neun nicht klappt. Alles klar? Danke, Tschüs!

6
– Du kommst am Samstag zur Party, OK?
– Ja, sicher, deine neue Adresse habe ich, aber wie ich zu euch komme, weiß ich nicht.
– OK. Hast du einen Zettel da? Gut. Also, du fährst mit dem Bus Linie 4 vom Marktplatz. OK, Linie 4. Am Hallenbad steigst du aus.
– So, am Hallenbad.
– Du gehst geradeaus, bis du zur Kirche kommst.
– Mmm …
– Unser Haus ist gegenüber der Kirche. Falls du Schwierigkeiten hast, gebe ich dir die Telefonnummer. 661352.
– 661352.

7
Guten Abend, meine Damen und Herren. Der Wetterbericht für heute, Mittwoch, den 12. März. In Norddeutschland ist das Wetter noch kalt und regnerisch. Die Höchsttemperatur beträgt 4 Grad. Im Süden ist es stark bewölkt, aber wir erwarten keine Schneefälle in den Alpen vor Samstag. Im Rheinland bleibt es sehr kalt mit starkem Wind. Höchsttemperatur, 2 Grad. Im Osten haben Sie heute das schönste Wetter – sonnig und warm bis mindestens Freitag.

Listening
Transcript

8
Guten Morgen, meine Damen und Herren. In der Lebensmittelabteilung haben wir heute frische Champignons im Sonderangebot, nur DM 6,99 das Kilo, ja, DM 6,99 das Kilo. Apfelsinen aus Spanien kosten heute nur DM 1,99. Ja, zehn saftige, süße Apfelsinen nur DM 1,99. Computer-Preishits, meine Damen und Herren – für Anfänger und Profis bieten wir Heim-Computer zu DM 549. Ein IBM, mit 8kRAM, komplett nur DM 549. Sport- und Tennisschuhe sind heute bis zu 20% reduziert. Ja, DM 75, Sportschuhe von Adidas, Puma usw. DM 75.

9
– Hallo, Firma Müller.
– Hallo, hier ist die Sekretärin der Geschäftsleiterin der Firma Smith und Brown in Manchester. Frau Johnson möchte gern bei ihrem Besuch Ihren Geschäftsführern einige Geschenke mitbringen und bittet um Ratschläge.
– Ja, gut. Herr Müller hat eine Vorliebe für britischen Fußball und hätte gern ein Buch über die Geschichte und die Ursprünge des Fußballs in England.
– OK – das ist eine tolle Idee.
– Frau Meyer ... Moment mal ... ach ja, sie liebt Musik, vielleicht eine CD – besonders gern hört sie klassische Musik. Vielleicht eine CD von einem englischen Komponisten.
– Und etwas für Herrn Krause, oder?
– Naja, das ist ganz einfach. Er ißt gern Pralinen, aber ... er ist auf Diät. Nun, er kocht auch gern ... vielleicht ein Buch mit englischen Kochrezepten?
– Dann bleibt nur noch Frau Decker, nicht wahr?
– Ja, sie trinkt besonders gern Tee, am liebsten englischen Tee. Da die Engländer Tee lieben, könnte Frau Johnson vielleicht eine typische englische Teekanne mitbringen.
– Alles klar. Vielen Dank für Ihre Hilfe. Auf Wiederhören.

10
– Guten Tag. Kann ich Ihnen helfen?
– Ja, ich habe meinen Rucksack im Zug vergessen.
– Welcher Zug war das?
– Der D-Zug aus Hamburg. Er ist eben weitergefahren.
– Wie sieht der Rucksack aus?
– Er ist dunkelgrün und hat braune Streifen.
– Gut, wir rufen beim Münchner Hauptbahnhof an, und Sie kommen am besten morgen nochmal vorbei.

11
– Ich heiße Klaus. Ich weiß nicht so genau, was ich machen werde. Ich werde vielleicht sofort arbeiten gehen. Ich möchte sofort gut verdienen.
– Ich heiße Martina. Ich werde einen Ausbildungsplatz suchen. Ich möchte Arzthelferin werden.
– Ich heiße Ute. Ich möchte nicht sofort arbeiten gehen. Für mich ist es, glaube ich, besser weiterzulernen, und dann das Abitur zu machen. Vielleicht sogar später auf die Universität zu gehen.
– Ich heiße Manfred. Ich interessiere mich nicht so sehr für Bücher und Schule. Ich möchte als Mechaniker arbeiten.
– Ich heiße Ulrike. Für mich ist eine berufliche Ausbildung am besten. Deshalb habe ich mich für eine Berufsschule entschieden.
– Ich heiße Reinhard. Mein Traum war immer, Journalist zu werden. Dazu brauche ich eine bessere Qualifikation, also bleibe ich noch länger in der Schule und mache das Abitur.
– Ich heiße Karl. Ich habe Glück, denn ich habe schon einen Job bei meinem Vater in seiner Firma. Da fange ich schon in einigen Wochen an.

12
– Petra hat Erfolg und bekommt eine Lehrstelle als Verkäuferin in einem großen Kaufhaus. Wir stellen einige Fragen über ihre Arbeit und ihre Zukunft. Wie stellst du dir eigentlich deine Zukunft vor?
– Das Wichtigste ist für mich jetzt meine Lehre. Ich verdiene nicht viel Geld, aber mir macht mein Beruf sehr viel Spaß. Ich versuche, zu meinen Kunden immer nett und freundlich zu sein. Ich habe jetzt schon einige Kunden, die zu mir kommen. Die wollen nur von mir bedient werden. Und das macht mich stolz und selbstsicher. Mein Traum für die Zukunft wäre, mit zwei, drei Leuten später mal eine Boutique aufzumachen. Man kann dann selbständiger arbeiten.
– Jetzt möchtest du aber erst mal deine Lehre fertig machen?
– Ja, in einem Großkaufhaus erhält man wirklich eine gute Ausbildung. Man kann viele Lehrgänge besuchen und sich weiterbilden. Das ist für mich sehr wichtig. Nächstes Jahr habe ich meine erste Prüfung, danach muß ich noch weiter lernen und Erfahrung sammeln. Und dann kommt die Hauptprüfung.
– Wie geht es dann weiter?
– In einem Großkaufhaus werden die meisten Ausgebildeten nach der Lehre fest angestellt. Auch ich hätte dann wahrscheinlich keine Probleme, hier einen Arbeitsplatz zu finden.

13
Ich war eine Woche bei meinem Onkel in der Autowerkstatt. Ich habe die ganze Woche Autos repariert und habe auch Autos gewaschen. Ich habe jeden Tag von halb acht bis vier Uhr gearbeitet. Es hat mir sehr gut gefallen.

14
Guten Morgen, Michael. Heute gibt es viel zu tun. Machen Sie bitte eine Liste, denn ich bin um halb zehn verabredet und kann Sie nicht vor fünf Uhr wiedersehen. Zuerst öffnen Sie die Briefe für Frau Gerling. Dann gibt es einige Dokumente zu fotokopieren. Nach der Kaffeepause tippen Sie bitte diesen Brief am Computer. Nehmen Sie die Mittagspause von halb zwölf bis halb eins. Danach könnten Sie Herrn Fischer anrufen. Fragen Sie ihn, um wieviel Uhr er morgen ankommen wird. Um vier Uhr bringen Sie die Briefe zur Post, und danach ist Feierabend. Sie können nach Hause gehen.

15
– Wann fahren wir?
– In den Herbstferien. Ende Oktober.
– Gut. Wir wohnen im Hotel?
– Was? Im Hotel! Nein, es gibt eine sehr gute Jugendherberge im Stadtzentrum und in der Nähe einer U-Bahnstation.
– Es ist praktischer und auch billiger!
– Was machen wir da?
– Alles Mögliche. Wir müssen uns die Sehenswürdigkeiten ansehen, ins Museum gehen und wenn wir Zeit haben, können wir vielleicht in die Eishalle oder ins Kino gehen.
– Berlin hat auch ein Hard Rock Café. Susi war letztes Jahr dort. Die Atmosphäre war super.

16
Hier ist Ihre Telefon-Info vom Verkehrsbüro Boppard. In Boppard können Sie Ausflüge mit dem Schiff nach Koblenz oder Rüdesheim machen. Morgen findet eine Sonderfahrt nach Rüdesheim statt – ab Boppard um um neun Uhr. Oder Sie können mit dem Zug nach Buchholz fahren.
Eine Stadtrundfahrt mit dem Rheinexpreß geht jeden Tag alle zwanzig Minuten zwischen 10.20 Uhr und 18.00 Uhr von der Karmeliter-Straße ab. Eine Stadtführung zu Fuß gibt es Dienstagnachmittag um 15.00 Uhr ab dem Verkehrsbüro in der Oberstraße. Mit dem Sessellift kommen Sie zum Vierseenblick. Oben angekommen, können Sie im Wald spazieren gehen und im Café Kaffee trinken. Für Informationen über Hotels rufen Sie bitte die Nummer 38 88 in Boppard an. Vorwahl 0 67 42.

17
– Guten Abend. Willkommen im Hotel Rheinblick. Kann ich Ihnen helfen?
– Ja, ich habe ein Zimmer für heute nacht reserviert. Mein Name ist Weiert.
– Weiert, Weiert … ach, ja. Ein Einzelzimmer mit Dusche, für zwei Nächte.
– Nein, das stimmt nicht. Ich wollte das Zimmer für drei Nächte.
– Ach, ja. Sie haben Recht. Bitte unterschreiben Sie hier … Danke schön. Also, Sie haben Zimmer 35. Es ist im dritten Stock. Sie haben Glück, dieses Zimmer hat einen schönen Blick auf den Rhein. Ihr Schlüssel, bitte. Ich wünsche Ihnen einen guten Aufenthalt. Der Aufzug ist hier links.

Part 3
1
– Also, was ist an der Schule gut oder schlecht?
– Ha, alles!
– Manche Lehrer sind total gut drauf, manche auch total mies. Zum Beispiel, wir haben so 'nen Lehrer auf der Schule, da machst du überhaupt nichts. An einem Tag machst du bei ihm nichts falsch, machst überhaupt nichts, dann schreit er plötzlich los: Was hast du gemacht? Und dann ist er voll sauer, und das ist unerträglich. Der ist der schlimmste Lehrer, den wir haben. Es gibt aber auch ziemlich coole Lehrer. Also, da dürfen wir uns zum Beispiel in Religion selber ein Thema aussuchen. Es ist ziemlich locker, und das macht eigentlich viel mehr Spaß als bei den Lehrern, wo es ziemlich streng zugeht.
– Ich finde, in manchen Situationen müssen die Lehrer so streng sein, aber bei uns auf der Schule ist's so schlimm, daß die Schüler machen, was sie wollen. Bei uns in der Klasse ist es sehr schlimm, wir sind die schlimmste Klasse auf der ganzen Schule, und … ähm … das ist ganz schlimm, die Lehrer kommen schon gar nicht mehr gegen die Schüler an. Also, sie machen einfach, was sie wollen. Zum Beispiel in Englisch. Bei uns ist der Lehrer sehr … gelassen. Bei uns im Unterricht klappt es nicht so gut. Deshalb machen wir eigentlich schon gar nicht mehr richtig Englisch.
– Mehr Deutsch. So wie die Lehrer, manche Lehrer, es gestalten, macht es überhaupt keinen Spaß. Wenn sie es interessanter gestalten würden, würden wir viel mehr mitarbeiten. Also, manche Lehrer machen das so schlaff. Sie sagen zum Beispiel: Was ist das? Was heißt das? Und wo liegt das? Kapiert man überhaupt gar nichts.
– Also, bei uns macht jetzt ein Lehrer, … ähm … also

Listening
Transcript

ein Englischlehrer bei uns, nimmt jetzt ein Lied durch, „Wind of Change" von den Scorpions. Also, es macht eigentlich schon Spaß, mehr Spaß als der Unterricht vorher.
– Also, Englisch ist so schwer zu begreifen halt, weil die Grammatik so kompliziert ist. Die Lehrer erklären das eben schlecht, und du verstehst überhaupt nichts. Die erklären das manchmal so kompliziert. Da wird das zum Beispiel in die Vergangenheit gesetzt, und du weißt nicht, warum das in die Vergangenheit gesetzt wird. Die reden halt so 'nen Kram. Du verstehst also überhaupt nichts. Manchmal reden sie nur deutsch, manchmal reden sie mehr englisch, dann verstehst du total Bahnhof und kapierst überhaupt nichts.

2
– Richard, seit wann rauchst du?
– Ich glaub', ich war so 10 oder 11. Wir waren damals so 'ne richtige Rasselbande. Wir wollten nur Unsinn machen. Und dann hat einer eine Zigarettenschachtel 'rumgereicht. Geschmeckt hat's nicht, aber Mann, wir haben uns gut gefühlt. Wie die Kings.
– Karin, wie war es mit dir?
– Bei mir war es die Schulfreundin. Ich war 13 Jahre alt. Mit der Kippe zwischen den Fingern fühlten wir uns eben erwachsen und attraktiv.
– Günter, wie alt warst du, als du angefangen hast?
– 14 Jahre. Ich wollte wie die andern sein und habe meine ersten Zigaretten einfach gekauft! Aber jetzt rauche ich nicht mehr. Und seit ich nicht rauche, bin ich einfach viel fitter. Ich huste jetzt nicht mehr, ich kann auch joggen gehen. Ich rieche und schmecke auch viel mehr.

3
– Würdest du Drogen probieren, Jan?
– Nein, erstens ist es illegal und zweitens ist es sehr gefährlich, weil man davon abhängig werden kann.
– Kennst du Leute, die Drogen nehmen?
– Ja, manche aus meiner Klasse machen das. Sie tun es, weil sie sich langweilen, weil es Spaß macht, oder weil es so viel Streß in der Schule gibt. Ich glaube, sie sind schwach und finden es halt schwierig, „nein" zu sagen.

4
– Das Brot in England hat mir gar nicht geschmeckt. Es ist weich und schmeckt nach nichts.
– Das stimmt. Bei unserem Bäcker gibt es 14 verschiedene Sorten von Brot. Aber in England habe ich höchstens drei oder vier Sorten gesehen – und kein Schwarzbrot oder Roggenbrot.

– Ich bin wenigstens in England nicht verhungert! Das war bei meiner Familie nicht möglich. Auch wenn das Brot so schlecht war. Es hat immer sehr viel zu essen gegeben. Aber trotzdem hätte ich mal gern ein paar gute deutsche Brötchen zum Frühstück gegessen.
– Das Gemüse in England war aber nicht so schlecht. Es ist viel gesünder als in Deutschland, weil es nicht so lange gekocht wird und deswegen noch alle Vitamine hat.
– Bäh!
– Doch, doch. In Deutschland wird zu viel Fleisch gegessen und dafür zu wenig Gemüse. Meine englische Gastmutter sagte immer: Gemüse ist gesund – aber nur, wenn es nicht zu lange gekocht wird.
– Meine englische Familie war vegetarisch und hat überhaupt kein Fleisch gegessen. Ich war drei Wochen dort und habe kein Roast Beef bekommen – aber gutes Gemüse und gute Salate schon.
– Bei uns hat es so oft fettige Pommes gegeben, weil die Kinder sonst keine Kartoffeln essen würden.
– Hm, Pommes mag ich ganz besonders.
– Aber zu viel Fett ist nicht gesund. Da habe ich immer gestaunt. Mrs Robinson war immer scharf auf gesundes Gemüse, und trotzdem gab es die ungesunden Pommes.
– Ja, wir essen zu Hause immer viel Fleisch, weil mein Onkel einen Bauernhof hat und selbst Schweine züchtet. In der Tiefkühltruhe gibt es immer alles vom Schwein. Schnitzel könnten wir jeden Tag bekommen. Letzte Woche hat er uns aber ein halbes Reh gebracht. Reh esse ich immer gern. Lecker! Besonders mit 'ner guten Soße.

5
Ein bewaffneter Mann hat die 64jährige Geschäftsführerin eines Ladens überfallen und dabei rund DM 800 geraubt. Der Unbekannte betrat kurz vor 13 Uhr den Laden und sagte, er wolle Geld wechseln. Der Mann war etwa 35 Jahre alt, 1,70 m groß und schlank. Er trug eine Sonnenbrille mit auffallend großen Gläsern. Sein roter Schnurrbart war vermutlich angeklebt.

6
– Ich komme sehr gut mit meiner Mutter aus. Wir reden eigentlich über alles, und sie ist gar nicht streng. Aber mein Vater ist ganz anders – er ist kaum zu Hause und hat nie Zeit für mich.
– Bei mir ist es umgekehrt – meine Mutter ist immer schlecht gelaunt, und ich muß viel zu Hause helfen. Mein Vater ist ganz lustig, und wir interessieren uns beide für Sport.

7
Abschnitt 1
- Also, Manfred, ich war gestern abend in der Oper. Die Aufführung war großartig.
- Na ja, Tante Hildegard, Opern … davon bin ich ja nicht gerade begeistert. Die Stimmen sind ja furchtbar – man versteht ja nun wirklich kein Wort davon.
- Was für Musik hörst du denn normalerweise, Manfred? Wohl diese Popmusik, oder?
- Na klar! Was denn sonst?
- Ach, das ist doch überhaupt keine richtige Musik. Die Sänger von heute schreien nur – das kann man nicht Musik nennen.

Abschnitt 2
- Ja, nun … ich gebe zu, es gibt Gruppen, die keine gute Musik machen, aber da gibt es auch andere Gruppen, die tolle Sachen bringen, bei denen richtige Texte vorkommen … die meinetwegen was zu sagen haben, übers Leben, über die Umwelt und so. Zum Beispiel R.E.M. oder Nirvana … die machen tolle Musik.
- Das sagst du.
- Doch, sie schreiben prima Texte.
- Tja, mag wohl sein … Aber weißt du, ich meine, ein großer Teil von dieser Musik, die wird in fünf, höchstens zehn Jahren völlig vergessen sein. Die Opern dagegen sind zum Teil schon hundert Jahre alt und werden immer noch aufgeführt.
- Aber ich finde, man merkt auch, daß sie hundert Jahre alt sind. Bei uns Jugendlichen kommen sie doch gar nicht an.
- Ja, ihr Jugendliche solltet der Kultur gegenüber ein bißchen offener sein.
- Aber, Tante Hildegard, das sind wir doch.

8
- Hört mal alle her! Nächstes Wochenende müssen wir etwas ganz Besonderes machen, bevor unser Gast nach Hause fährt.
- Ich hätte einen Vorschlag. Im Theater wird ein gutes Stück gespielt. Wie wäre es damit?
- Ja, aber unser englischer Gast würde wahrscheinlich nicht alles verstehen. Wie wäre es denn mit dem Rockkonzert in der Stadthalle am Samstag?
- Ach! Das ist doch nichts für die ältere Generation! Das soll doch ein Familienausflug sein! Also, ich schlage vor, wir fahren an den Bodensee, und dort können wir auch übernachten. Das wäre doch was!
- Ja, und wir könnten einen Ausflug mit dem Boot machen. Der Bodensee ist sehr schön. Es ist zwar ein bißchen teuer, aber ich glaube, das ist eine gute Idee.

9
- Mein Name ist Michael. Ich komme gut mit meinen Eltern aus. Sie sind locker, und ich mache meistens, was ich will. Das heißt, sie vertrauen mir, ich bin alt genug zu wissen, was richtig ist. Wenn ich Probleme habe, kann ich immer mit ihnen reden.
- Ich bin der Ralf. Ich habe auch keine Schwierigkeiten mit meinen Eltern. Ich darf bis Mitternacht ausgehen. In meinem Alter geht das. Mein Vater ist sowieso meistens weg von zu Hause mit seiner Arbeit. Wir machen nicht viel zusammen als Familie.
- Ich heiße Barbara. Ihr habt Glück, ihr Jungen! Ich muß immer meinen Eltern sagen, wohin ich gehe, mit wem, wann ich zurückkomme. Überhaupt kein Privatleben! Ich darf nicht meine Klammotten alleine kaufen. Meine Mutter sagt, sie hat ein Recht, weil sie das Geld ausgibt.
- Ich heiße Anja. Ich muß meinen Eltern auch sagen, um wieviel Uhr ich nach Hause komme, aber das find' ich total normal. Mein Problem ist meine Geige. Sie meinen, ich muß jeden Tag das dumme Ding üben und sind sehr streng mit mir. Meine Mutter und ich gehen oft schwimmen oder Tennis spielen. Wir mögen beide sehr gerne Sport, aber das ist nichts für meinen Vater.

10
1
Abschnitt 1
Die Leute aus Norddeutschland können sich den Karneval nie vorstellen. Vor einigen Jahren kam meine Schwester Ingeborg aus Norddeutschland hierher, und ich sagte zu ihr: Wir gehen heute nachmittag zum Karnevalszug. Das war der Sonntag vor Rosenmontag. Da hatte meine Schwester nichts dagegen, und als wir losgingen, da steckte ich ihr ein paar Luftballons in die Hand und habe ihr einen lustigen Hut gegeben. Sie guckte etwas unsicher, aber protestierte nicht, da gingen wir in die Stadt.

Abschnitt 2
Und Ingeborg sah, daß hier aus der ganzen Stadt jede Menge Leute zum Markt liefen, und alle trugen Kostüme. Wir waren bei der Kirche am Markt, und dann bin ich mit ihr mitten auf der Straße – da war noch keine Fußgängerzone – Arm in Arm bis zur katholischen Kirche gegangen. Und da hat sie gesehen, daß die ganze Straße voll war von närrischem Volk. Und dann sagte sie ganz überrascht: Die Leute spielen hier richtig mit. Ich sagte: Ja, das ist ein Volksfest, etwas Echtes. Es geschieht auch wirklich, nicht nur im Fernsehen.

Listening
Transcript

2
- Gefällt dir die Stadt, Anna?
- Ich wohne am Rande der Stadt – nur ungefähr eine halbe Stunde vom Zentrum entfernt. Ich kann leicht mit dem Fahrrad in die Stadt fahren. Ich kann also beides haben, Stadt und Land.
- Was meinst du dazu, Boris?
- Jetzt wohnen wir im Dorf. Wir sind letztes Jahr aus der Stadt hierher gezogen. Es ist stinklangweilig hier. Ich muß immer sehr lange mit dem Bus fahren, um Freunde zu treffen.

3
- Du wohnst auf dem Land, und du hast einen Freund, der in der Großstadt lebt, also in Bremen. Gestaltet er seine Freizeit anders im Vergleich zu euch?
- Auf jeden Fall. Bei uns ist es meistens so, daß wir in der Stadt suchen müssen, um großartig was zu finden. Also, ich wohne mitten auf dem Land, da muß ich mit dem Fahrrad fahren, und es dauert schon eine Dreiviertelstunde, bis ich in der Stadt bin. Bei meinem Freund in Bremen ist es so: Er geht zur Bushaltestelle, und in fünf Minuten ist er in der Stadt, und er kann überall hingehen. Da ist die Infrastruktur viel besser – Straßenbahn und so. Und ja, was macht er – Tanzkurs. Es gibt viel mehr Angebote. Für uns auf dem Lande ist es nicht so einfach. Wir müssen in die Stadt fahren, aber wenn man kein eigenes Auto hat, dann geht man einfach nicht hin, oder die Eltern bringen einen dahin. Oder man fährt mit dem Fahrrad, bloß im Winter ist es ziemlich blöd, wenn man so über eine halbe Stunde beim schönsten Schneesturm mit dem Fahrrad fahren muß – oder man bleibt einfach zu Hause.

11

1 Es ist mir eigentlich egal, was gerade Mode ist. Ich trage immer, was mir gefällt. Am liebsten sportliche Sachen – ich kriege oft Kleider von meiner Schwester, oder ich kaufe mir Klamotten auf dem Markt.

2 Der Apfelkuchen. Zuerst braucht man natürlich die Äpfel, 500 g. Was sonst? Also, für den Teig mußt du 200 g Mehl und 200 g Butter kaufen, verstehst du das? 200 g Mehl und Butter. Und dann muß man zwei Eier haben … und eine Zitrone, ja, eine schöne Zitrone. Ist das alles? Ach nein, Zucker natürlich … etwa 100 g Zucker insgesamt. Also, hast du das dann? Äpfel … Mehl … Butter … Eier … Zitrone … und Zucker. Alles klar?

3
- Nächste Woche hat Vati Geburtstag. Was schenken wir ihm?
- Ich weiß nicht. Jedes Jahr dasselbe Problem. Übrigens bin ich im Moment pleite, weißt du?
- Wie wär's mit neuen Handschuhen? Seine sind uralt.
- Ja, … ähm … aber Handschuhe aus Leder – ist das nicht schrecklich teuer?
- Ach, zu teuer – könnte sein. Ja, vielleicht, zu teuer. Wir könnten auch eine Armbanduhr kaufen, oder?
- Ja, aber er trägt sehr gerne die, die Opa ihm geschenkt hat.
- Ja, ja. Er trägt sie immer, nicht wahr? Sie gefällt ihm sehr gut, diese alte Armbanduhr von seinem Vater.
- Was meinst du? Er braucht einen neuen Gürtel.
- Nein, das ist keine gute Idee, er hat einen.
- Der ist auch sehr alt, und weißt du was? Letzte Woche hab' ich ihn im Kaufhaus gesehen, und er guckte sich die neuen Gürtel an.
- Toll, dann schenken wir ihm einen nagelneuen Gürtel, oder?
- Abgemacht! Eine super Idee! Ja, prima!

12

1
- Und wie sind Sie mit dem Verkehr zurechtgekommen? Nach meiner Erfahrung gewöhnt man sich relativ schnell an den Linksverkehr.
- Bei mir war es so – jedesmal, wenn ein Freund mich fahren wollte, dann stieg ich an der Seite ein, wo der Fahrersitz war.
- Was halten Sie denn von den öffentlichen Verkehrsmitteln in England? Die sind, meiner Meinung nach, nicht so gut wie in Deutschland.
- Das finde ich nicht. Das Verkehrsnetz ist wesentlich besser als in Deutschland. Ich meine, die Busse fahren … vielleicht nicht häufiger…, aber sie fahren bis in die entferntesten Dörfer. Man kann auch viel preiswerter mit Bussen oder Zügen fahren als hier bei uns.
- Aber in einigen Fällen ließ die Sauberkeit von den Bussen und Zügen zu wünschen übrig. Und außerdem kamen sie ab und zu mit mehreren Minuten Verspätung an.

2 Heute morgen ist bei einem schweren Verkehrsunfall auf der Autobahnstrecke Ulm-Augsburg eine Frau getötet worden. Vier Menschen wurden schwer verletzt. Ein Personenwagen ist mit einem Tankwagen zusammengestoßen. Dann ist der Tankwagen in einen zweiten Personenwagen gefahren. 18 000 Liter Öl sind aus dem Tankwagen ausgelaufen. Die Polizei mußte die Autobahn für vier Stunden sperren.

13

1 Ich bin jetzt 16 Jahre alt und in der 10. Klasse. Ich möchte noch bis zur 13. Klasse am Gymnasium bleiben und das Abitur machen. Nach dem Abitur möchte ich gern als Au-pair-Mädchen nach Frankreich gehen und dort in einer französischen Familie arbeiten und die Sprache richtig lernen. Der Au-pair-Job dauert ein Jahr. Und Englisch kann ich ganz gut, denn ich bin, wie du weißt, ganz oft in England. Danach möchte ich mit dem Studium anfangen – wahrscheinlich Englisch und Französisch. Ich möchte gern Lehrerin für Fremdsprachen werden. Dafür müßte ich fünf Jahre studieren und ein Jahr an der Schule auf Probe unterrichten. Ich habe mal im Kindergarten als Aushilfe gearbeitet, und die Arbeit mit den Kindern hat mir viel Spaß gemacht.

2
- Das Krankenhaus Bonn sucht Krankenschwestern und Krankenpfleger für Tag- und Nachtdienst.
- Tommis Fahrschule sucht ab sofort zwei Fahrlehrer mit guten Qualifikationen.

3
Monika
- Ich habe immer mit alten Leuten arbeiten wollen, und das will ich immer noch.
- Wie lange warst du im Altersheim?
- Ich war zwei Wochen da. Jetzt aber werde ich jeden Samstagmorgen drei Stunden lang arbeiten.

Georg
- Ja, ich habe auch gute Erfahrungen mit dem Berufspraktikum gemacht.
- Wo warst du denn?
- Im Hotel. Ich habe in der Küche gearbeitet. Zwei Wochen waren genug für mich! Es war so hektisch. Aber die Leute waren so freundlich. Ich würde gerne das nächste Mal auch da arbeiten, nur in der Küche nicht.

Markus
Ich wollte überhaupt kein Berufspraktikum machen und ich hatte recht! Ich mußte jeden Morgen um 6.30 Uhr aufstehen und bin erst gegen 6 Uhr abends wieder nach Hause gekommen. Ich habe im Supermarkt gearbeitet, es war schrecklich – nie wieder!

4
Vor zwei Jahren bin ich nach Deutschland gekommen. Ich arbeite im Moment bei einer Versicherungsfirma im Stadtzentrum. Die Arbeit beginnt um acht Uhr – eine Stunde früher als in England – aber das gefällt mir gut, weil ich schon um halb vier oder fünf Uhr nach Hause gehen kann. Ich wohne aber ganz am Rande der Stadt, und die Fahrt zur Arbeit dauert sehr lange. Aber ich finde die Kollegen sehr nett und hilfsbereit. Die Arbeit selbst ist ziemlich uninteressant, und ich hoffe, im September mit einer Informatik-Ausbildung anzufangen.

5
Die Not der Kollegen war groß damals. Wir arbeiteten damals 54 Stunden in der Woche. Urlaub? Wir hatten so sechs bis acht Tage Urlaub im Jahr. Erst 1948 bin ich zum ersten Mal mit meiner Frau in den Urlaub gefahren. Und der Lohn, also, ich bekam damals zwischen 250 und 300 Mark brutto, sehr wenig. An ein Auto oder Motorrad dachte damals kein Mensch, und wir aßen meistens Margarine. Butter war teuer, ja viel zu teuer für uns. Heutzutage essen wir Butter, soviel wir wollen, und wir haben zwar ein Auto und einen Farbfernseher, aber die Familie, die ist heute nicht so eng. Die Familie war damals wichtiger, die Familie war stärker damals, und die Familie ist eben viel wichtiger, nicht?

14

Hallo, Frau Müller am Apparat, im Auftrag der Firma Müller in Hamburg. Ich telefoniere betreffs des Besuchs im nächsten Monat von Frau Johnson. Wir haben für sie ein Zimmer in einem Hotel in einem Vorort gebucht, und zwar ungefähr 5 Kilometer vom Stadtzentrum. Es ist ein Einzelzimmer mit Bad und Dusche im ersten Stock. Vom Zimmer aus hat sie eine gute Aussicht auf die große Alster, einen großen See in Hamburg. Wir werden natürlich selber für das Zimmer bezahlen. Wenn Frau Johnson es will, versorgen wir sie auch während ihres Aufenthaltes mit einem Auto. Sie kommt für eine Woche, und wir haben für sie einen Besuch in einer Schule organisiert. Es wird auch eine Stadtbesichtigung geben, wo sie alle Sehenswürdigkeiten sehen wird. Wir glauben, Frau Johnson interessiert sich für Oper, und an einem Abend gehen wir zu einer Oper im Hamburger Stadttheater. Auf dem Programm steht eine Oper von dem deutschen Komponisten Weber. Bitte rufen Sie uns zurück, um alles zu bestätigen. Sagen Sie uns bitte gleichzeitig, ob sie das Auto haben möchte, und ob sie andere Freizeitwünsche hat. Da wir außerdem für ihre Mahlzeiten im Hotel und in der Betriebskantine zuständig sein werden, teilen Sie uns bitte mit, ob Frau Johnson besondere Eßwünsche hat. Vielen Dank im voraus. Auf Wiederhören.

15

Fahr in Urlaub nach Südfrankreich! Genieße Strand und Meer!

Listening
Transcript

16

1. Guten Tag, meine Damen und Herren. Ich heiße Brigitte Fehst und bin Ihre Stadtführerin. Die ganze Tour wird etwa 90 Minuten dauern. Ausgangspunkt ist das Verkehrsamt, und am Ende genießen wir die Atmosphäre der Altstadt.

2. Gegen 13.00 Uhr werden wir in einem traditionellen Gasthaus in der Altstadt zu Mittag essen. Die Kosten dafür sind schon im Preis der Führung enthalten.

3. Zuerst besichtigen wir den Dom. Von dort kommen wir zum Römisch-Germanischen Museum mit seiner berühmten Glassammlung, den Mosaiken und den Resten der römischen Mauer.
   Gleich daneben befindet sich die neue Philharmonie, Kölns größter Konzertsaal. Hier können bis zu 2000 Besucher bekannte Orchester aus aller Welt hören.
   Zum Abschluß gehen wir auf eine der großen Brücken über den Rhein, die elegante Deutzer-Brücke. Von hier aus können Sie einen wunderschönen Blick auf die Altstadt genießen.

17

Also, das Park Hotel war kein erstklassiges Hotel, sondern das Letzte! Mein Zimmer war winzig – und hatte weder Bad noch Dusche! Ich sage dir, es gab kein Bad und keine Dusche im Zimmer. Alle Zimmer verfügen über Telefon, Radio und Farbfernseher, so heißt es. Also, ich hatte zwar ein Telefon, aber der Farbfernseher war kaputt. Kaputt, sag' ich dir. Kein Bild, nichts! Tischtennis und Billard gab es nicht. Das Spielzimmer war noch nicht fertig, also konnten wir nicht Tischtennis spielen. Und das Essen … das Essen am Abend war das Schlimmste – keine Auswahl und kleine Portionen. Wir hatten nie ein viergängiges Menü, nie. Meistens gab es nur ein Hauptgericht und Nachtisch, und dann meistens nur etwas mit Pommes und Eis als Nachtisch. Was für eine Woche …

18

– Was macht ihr für die Umwelt?
– Was wir bei uns in der Familie machen? Ja – wir sortieren den Müll. Das ist alles, glaube ich.
– Was? Nein, du fährst nicht immer mit dem Auto in die Schule. Die meiste Zeit fährst du mit dem Rad, und gehst ab und zu, zu Fuß.
– Wir senken die Temperatur im Haus um 2°. Es spart nicht nur Energie, sondern auch Geld.
– Wenn wir zum Supermarkt gehen, kaufen wir oft Ökoprodukte. Die sind manchmal teurer, aber … was noch? Wir kaufen keine Produkte mit zu viel Verpackungsmaterial.
– Das größte Problem für die Umwelt in Deutschland sind Autos. Wir haben zu viele Autos, sie verpesten die Luft und sind auch so laut.

Solutions: Speaking

Area A

2
Rôle-play B *(page 63)*

Lehrer(in): Du bist bei deiner Brieffreundin in Deutschland. Ich bin dein(e) Freund(in).

Also, nach dem Abendessen gehen wir zur Party bei Thorsten.

Du: Um wieviel Uhr ist das Abendessen? [a]

Lehrer(in): Gegen halb acht.

Du: Ich möchte mir die Haare waschen. [b]

Lehrer(in): Okay, gute Idee, ich auch. Wie lange bist du im Badezimmer?

Du: Oh, nur zehn Minuten. [c]

Lehrer(in): Gut, ich gehe nachher.

Du: Wann kommen wir nach Hause? [d]

Lehrer(in): Nicht zu spät. Mitternacht vielleicht.

[a] Another way of asking this would be *Wann essen wir heute abend?*

[b] You could also use *darf ich* (may I) or *ich will* (I want to).

[c] Any suitable length of time will do here.

[d] You could also say *Um wieviel Uhr sind wir wieder zu Hause?*

3
Rôle-play A *(page 68)*

Lehrer(in): Sie sind beim Zahnarzt in Deutschland. Ich bin der Zahnarzt.

Guten Tag. Was kann ich für Sie tun?

Du: Guten Tag, ich bin Engländer, ich heiße John. [a]

Lehrer(in): Ja, und was fehlt Ihnen?

Du: Ich habe schreckliche Zahnschmerzen [b] **seit zwei Tagen.** [c]

Lehrer(in): Ach, so. Und was machen Sie hier in Deutschland?

Du: Ich bin hier im Urlaub mit einer deutschen Familie. [d]

Lehrer(in): So, es ist nicht schlimm, ich kann Ihnen helfen.

Du: Danke.

[a] You could also say, *Ich komme aus England/Irland/Schottland/Wales.*

[b] Be sure to learn the whole range of aches and pains, many of which end in *-schmerzen* e.g. sore throat – *Halsschmerzen*, stomach-ache – *Magenschmerzen*.

[c] The preposition *seit* is used with a time and the present tense to say how long something has been going on, e.g. *Ich habe Fieber seit drei Stunden.* (I've had a temperature for three hours.)

[d] There is a range of possibilities here and you have to be prepared to respond spontaneously. Watch out for the symbol warning you about an unpredictable question in the Foundation/Higher rôle-play. You could have said *Ich mache einen Austausch/Ich wohne bei einer deutschen Familie/Ich bin mit meiner Familie im Urlaub.* You could simply describe one of your activities: *Ich besuche die schönen Städte in der Gegend/Wir gehen jeden Tag zum Strand, um zu baden.* You can get points for any answer which makes sense in reply to the question – it isn't a trap to catch you out. The examiners want you to do well!

Solutions
Speaking

Rôle-play B *(page 69)*

Lehrer(in): Sie sind im Urlaub in Deutschland und müssen beim Arzt anrufen. Ich bin die Frau am Empfang.

Hier Sprechstunde Dr. Puls. Wie kann ich Ihnen helfen?

Du: Guten Tag.ᵃ Es geht mir nicht gut. Ich möchte heute einen Termin mit dem Arzt, bitte.ᵇ

Lehrer(in): Ach, wissen Sie, das ist schwierig. Was fehlt Ihnen denn?

Du: Ich habe Fieber und starke Magenschmerzen. Ich habe gar nicht geschlafen. Gestern hatte ich auch Durchfall.ᶜ

Lehrer(in): Ich kann Ihnen einen Termin für Dienstag um 8 Uhr geben. Geht das?

Du: Nein, das geht nicht. Ich muß morgen nach Hause nach England fliegen. Ich weiß nicht, ob ich fahren kann.ᵈ

Lehrer(in): Schwierig … Kommen Sie am besten sofort vorbei.

Du: Danke schön. Ich werde in zwanzig Minuten bei Ihnen sein.ᵉ

Lehrer(in): Wie heißen Sie?

Du: John Forsyth.

Lehrer(in): Ja, Herr Forsyth, können Sie Ihren Namen buchstabieren, bitte.

Du: F-O-R-S-Y-T-H. ᶠ

Lehrer(in): Danke schön. Also, bis gleich, Herr Forsyth.

a Remember to play along with the rôle. In this situation you must be very polite.

b Using a phrase like *Ich möchte …* with the verb correctly positioned at the end, is a good polite way to ask for something.

c You can really show off here, by having several symptoms ready, The answer is really good because it brings in a past tense by talking about yesterday's symptoms.

d A good answer; not only have you remembered about the detail that you must go home tomorrow, but you have brought in an opinion to support the urgency of your case.

e An excellent answer, using a future tense, which will really impress the examiner.

f This unpredictable question is often used (sometimes you'll hear *Wie schreibt man das?*) so make sure you know your German alphabet really well.

5
Rôle-play A *(page 71)*

1

Lehrer(in): Sie wollen mit Freunden essen.

Bitte schön?

Du: Guten Tag. Haben Sie einen Tisch für vier Personen, bitte?

Lehrer(in): Ja, bitte schön. Was möchten Sie bestellen?

Du: Bratwurst, bitte.ᵃ

Lehrer(in): Mit Salzkartoffeln?

Du: Nein, mit Pommes frites, bitte.ᵇ

Lehrer(in): Und zu trinken?

Du: Eine Limonade,ᶜ bitte.ᵈ

Lehrer(in): Kommt sofort.

Du: Wo sind die Toiletten, bitte?ᵉ

Lehrer(in): Dort drüben.

a When you order you could use *Ich möchte Bratwurst, bitte* or *Haben Sie Bratwurst, bitte?* and, of course, *Bockwurst* or *Currywurst* would get full marks too.

b The third picture has a little catch because the teacher/waiter offers you *Salzkartoffeln* (boiled potatoes). Don't be misled by the … -*kartoffeln* and say *Ja, …* by mistake. Stick to the *Pommes frites* you had prepared beforehand.

c Your drink order could be *Orangensaft, Sprudel* or *Mineralwasser* and you could even add *Ein Glas …* if you want to.

d Note the use of *bitte* after each request, to keep the tone of the conversation polite.

e Your final question could be as short as *Die Toiletten, bitte?* to gain full marks.

Solutions
Speaking

2

Lehrer(in): Du bist mit deinen Eltern im Café in Deutschland. Ich bin der Kellner und spreche zuerst.

Guten Tag. Was möchten Sie bestellen?

Du: Ich möchte zwei Tassen Kaffee, bitte.^a

Lehrer(in): Sonst noch etwas?

Du: Ein Glas Cola, bitte.^b

Lehrer(in): Essen Sie etwas dazu?

Du: Haben Sie Kuchen?^c

Lehrer(in): Ja, wir haben Käsekuchen.

Du: Also, drei Stück Kuchen, bitte.^d

Lehrer(in): Danke. Kommt sofort.

Du: Was kostet das, bitte?^e

Lehrer(in): DM 22,90.

a Just saying what you want and adding *bitte* would get full marks, but using *Ich möchte …* is a much politer form.

b Keeping it simple carries no penalty in the Foundation tier as long as the message is fully understood.

c You could also use the more difficult phrase: *Was für Kuchen haben Sie?* (What sort of cakes do you have?) Both will earn full marks, so go for the one you feel confident with.

d Again you could add *Ich möchte …* or *Ich nehme …* or use a commonly-heard phrase *Dreimal Kuchen, bitte.* (Literally – Cake three times, please.)

e Here you have several possibilities: *Die Rechnung, bitte.* (The bill, please.); *Was macht das zusammen, bitte?* (How much is that all together, please?); *Ich möchte zahlen, bitte* or *Zahlen, bitte.* (I'd like to pay, please.). Remember then, that if you can't say what you want to say, you can usually find something else to say instead.

Rôle-play B *(page 72)*

2

Lehrer(in): Sie sind im Restaurant. Ich bin die Kellnerin.

Bitte schön?

Du: Haben Sie einen Tisch für zwei Personen, bitte?^a

Lehrer(in): Wo möchten Sie sitzen?

Du: Hier in der Ecke, bitte.^b

Lehrer(in): Ja, das geht.

Du: Kann ich bitte die Speisekarte haben?^c

Lehrer(in): Selbstverständlich.

Du: Wir möchten zwei Cola und zwei Käsebrote, bitte.^d

Lehrer(in): Gerne.

a Other possible responses include: *Ich möchte/Wir möchten einen Tisch für zwei Personen, bitte; Gibt es einen Tisch …*

b Other possible answers include: *Neben dem Fenster* (Near the window); *Hier vorne* (Just here); *Da hinten* (Over there at the back); *Oben* (Upstairs); *Unten* (Downstairs); *Auf der Terrasse* (On the terrace).

c You could also simply say: *Die Speisekarte, bitte.* And still get full marks.

d You have a free hand here to use any relevant food and drink you want to, so make sure they are ones you will get full marks for. There are many examples in *GCSE German Vocabulary* – *Zweimal Hähnchen, bitte und zwei Kännchen Kaffee. Als Nachtisch hätte ich gern ein Eis.* (Two portions of chicken, please and two pots of coffee. For desert I'd like an ice-cream.)

Solutions
Speaking

Conversation A *(page 73)*

1. Was trinkst du gern?

    Ich trinke sehr gern[a] Cola und Orangensaft.[b]

2. Was ißt du gern?

    Mein Lieblingsessen[c] ist Pizza.[d] Das esse ich sehr gerne.[e] Und Sie?[f]

3. Was ißt du zum Frühstück?

    Ich esse gewöhnlich Corn Flakes, Toast mit Marmelade, und ich trinke Milch.[g]

4. Wo ißt du normalerweise zu Mittag?

    Normalerweise esse ich in der Kantine.

5. Gefällt dir das, oder?

    Nein, es ist furchtbar! Ich kann es nicht leiden![h]

[a] Saying *Ich trinke* and adding *sehr gern* will impress the examiner more than simply *Cola und Orangensaft*.

[b] It's always better to give two examples rather than just one.

[c] This is an excellent answer because it uses different words from the teacher to answer the question.

[d] You will get just as many marks for a simple answer as for something complicated like *Pizza, Nudeln und Hamburger*.

[e] This emphasis is good, because it expresses your feelings about the food strongly. You can use the same phrase with a different verb in many places: *Das spiele ich sehr gern. Das lerne ich sehr gern.*

[f] It is always a good idea to ask the examiner a question and this is by far the easiest way to do it. Answer the question, then add to your answer *Und Sie?*

[g] A full answer with good examples of things to eat and the extra verb *Ich trinke* will earn extra credit.

[h] Adding your opinion *Ich kann es nicht leiden* (I can't stand it!) or *Ich kann es gut leiden* (It is all right) will always impress the examiners.

Conversation B *(page 73)*

1. Warst du schon in Deutschland?

    Nein, ich war noch nie in Deutschland.[a] Aber ich war letztes Jahr in Spanien,[b] und nächstes Jahr hoffe ich, nach Deutschland zu fahren.[c]

2. Was ist ein typisch deutsches Essen, deiner Meinung nach?

    Ich weiß nicht genau, aber vielleicht Wurst mit Sauerkraut und Salzkartoffeln? Die Deutschen essen viel Wurst, sagt man.[d]

3. Was wirst du heute abend essen?

    Heute abend esse ich wahrscheinlich[e] mein Lieblingsessen, Pizza mit Pommes frites. Als Nachtisch gibt es hoffentlich[e] Erdbeereis. Das schmeckt mir gut![f]

4. Beschreib bitte dein ideales Essen.

    Ja, ich habe mein ideales Essen letztes Wochenende gegessen.[g] Wir sind ins Restaurant gegangen, weil meine Mutti Geburtstag hatte.[h] Ich habe Hähnchen mit Reis gegessen. Und als Nachtisch gab es[i] Schwarzwälderkirschtorte. Wunderbar![j]

5. „Yorkshire pudding" – was ist das genau?

    Das ist eine Art Pfannkuchen. Die Zutaten[k] sind Eier, Mehl, Milch und Salz. Man ißt das gewöhnlich mit Rindfleisch. Es ist sehr gut![l]

[a] *Ich war noch nie in Deutschland.* You could say *Ich bin noch nie nach Deutschland gefahren*. Both are excellent examples of past tenses.

[b] It is a really good idea to follow your *Nein* with *aber* and to say something you have done.

[c] The reference to the future will score high marks, as will using the phrase *nächstes Jahr*. Always look out for the chance to say *nächstes Jahr hoffe ich …* and put your second verb at the end after *zu – Nächstes Jahr hoffe ich Biologie zu lernen.*

[d] You don't have to be an expert in everything, so don't be afraid to say *ich weiß nicht genau* (I don't know exactly) and to pass off general opinions with *man sagt* (they say).

[e] These two words, *wahrscheinlich* (probably) and *hoffentlich* (hopefully), will attract high marks by adding variety to simple sentences.

[f] A good opinion brought in with your own initiative.

[g] An excellent way to put the answer to a general question into the past tense.

[h] The use of *weil* with the verb in the correct position at the end will impress. Try to learn some examples of this and use them whenever you can.

[i] *Es gab* (There was/were) is the past tense of *es gibt*. It will help you to score well by adding another past tense to your repertoire.

[j] An easy way to add an opinion!

[k] *Die Zutaten sind* (the ingredients are) could be replaced by *Man macht das mit Eiern …*

[l] Another opinion introduced on your initiative.

Solutions
Speaking

Conversation C *(page 74)*

1 Was würdest du sagen, wenn ich dir Sauerkraut zu essen gäbe?

Es ist schwer zu sagen.ᵃ Ich habe Sauerkraut nie gegessen, aber ich möchte es (nicht) probieren.ᵇ Ich habe schon Bratwurst gegessen, und das schmeckt mir (nicht)ᵇ gut.ᶜ

2 Welche Gerichte kochst du selbst gern?

Was ich sehr gerne koche, ist Eintopf. Letztes Wochenende habe ich zum Beispiel einen großen Eintopf für die ganze Familie gekocht.ᵈ Darin waren Hackfleisch, Kartoffeln, Karotten, Pilze und Erbsen. Es war wirklich lecker!ᵉ

3 Sag mir, wie man einen Tisch decken sollte?

Also, bei uns deckt man den Tisch zuerst mit einem Tischtuch. Dann deckt man für jede Person ein Messer, eine Gabel, einen Löffel und ein Glas. Gestern abend, als ich den Tisch gedeckt habe, habe ich Salz und Pfeffer vergessen.ᶠ Mutti war nicht sehr zufrieden. Heute abend werde ich Salz und Pfeffer nicht vergessen.ᵍ

4 Was für ein Essen würdest du vorschlagen, wenn du einen deutschen Freund zu Besuch hättest?

Also, man sagtʰ, daß alle Fremden unseren Fisch mit Pommes frites essen wollen. Es gibt ein tolles Fischrestaurant, wo man sehr gut essen kann.ⁱ Ich würde mit meinem Freund dahingehen. Ich bin überzeugtʲ, daß ihm das gut schmecken würde, und es ist nicht zu teuer.

5 Was ist dein Lieblingsrestaurant?

Ach, ich habe kein Lieblingsrestaurant. Ich gehe sehr selten ins Restaurant, weil das so teuer ist.ᵏ Aber ich gehe manchmal mit meinen Freunden ins Café, wo wir Cola oder Kaffee trinken.ˡ

a This is a good phrase (It's difficult to say), which can give you time to think of an answer and, in any case, sounds very authentic even if you know exactly what you want to say.

b You can leave out the *nicht* and have the opposite meaning here.

c An excellent answer which brings in references to both the past and the future by using *ich möchte*.

d The use of *Zum Beispiel, letztes Wochenende...* with a past tense will always score highly.

e A good personal opinion freely given.

f The reference to the past with *Gestern abend* will attract good marks.

g The phrase *Ich werde nicht vergessen* (I won't forget) can be used in many situations and is well worth learning and using as a handy future reference.

h *Man sagt, daß ...* is an impressive phrase, especially with the verb in the correct place at the end.

i *Wo* can be used to good effect to join two ideas (or clauses) but remember to put the verb at the end of the clause.

j *Ich bin (davon) überzeugt* (I'm convinced (of it)) is an excellent way of expressing a strong opinion. You can use it in many conversations.

k An excellent opinion, backed up by a reason introduced by *weil*. You should always use a sentence like this in your conversation whenever you can.

l Here the use of *aber* with something you do like to do, gives a more positive feel to your answer after the earlier negative idea.

Area B

1
Conversation A *(page 75)*

1 Erzähl mir etwas von deiner Familie.

Ich wohne bei meiner Mutter und meinem Vater.

2 Was für Geschwister hast du?

Keine, ich bin ein Einzelkind. Aber ich habe eine kleine Katze, die sehr süß ist.

3 Was ist dein Lieblingshaustier?

Solutions
Speaking

Ja, meine Katze ist mein Lieblingshaustier. Katzen sind wirklich gut, sehr unabhängig.

4 Wann hast du Geburtstag?

Mein Geburtstag ist am neunzehnten Oktober.

5 Kannst du deinen besten Freund oder deine beste Freundin beschreiben?

Ja, er ist ziemlich groß und hat kurze, braune Haare.

> These are good answers, which will gain full marks in the Foundation tier. Note especially the extra point made in Number 3, expressing an opinion. Number 5 gives a full answer and the use of *ziemlich* (quite) will attract marks.

Conversation B *(page 75)*

1 Erzähl mir etwas von deiner Familie.

Also, ich wohne bei meinem Vater und meiner Stiefmutter. Meine Stiefmutter heißt Margaret, und ich komme gut mit ihr aus, weil sie immer gut gelaunt ist. Mein Vater ist groß und sehr ruhig.

2 Was für Geschwister hast du?

Keine, ich bin ein Einzelkind, aber ich habe einen Hund, der sehr komisch ist. Er ist braun und weiß, und er frißt alles, was er findet. Heute morgen, zum Beispiel, hat er das Frühstück von meinem Vater gefressen, als er sich ein Glas Milch holte.

3 Was ist dein Lieblingshaustier?

Mein Lieblingshaustier ist der Hund. Hunde sind fantastisch, man kann sich wirklich auf sie verlassen. Eines Tages werde ich hoffentlich mehrere Hunde haben. Das wird toll sein!

4 Wann hast du Geburtstag?

Mein Geburtstag ist am einundzwanzigsten September. Ich werde siebzehn. Dann darf ich abends länger ausbleiben und, noch besser, ich darf Autofahren lernen. Ich freue mich sehr darauf und spare für mein eigenes Auto.

5 Kannst du deinen besten Freund oder deine beste Freundin beschreiben?

Aber natürlich. Er ist ziemlich groß und stark mit kurzen dunklen Haaren. Wir haben viel Spaß zusammen, weil er selten schlecht gelaunt ist. Man kann sich auf ihn verlassen, weil er vernünftig und ruhig ist.

> If you compare the model answers for Foundation and Higher tiers, you will see how different the examiners' expectations are. Not only are the Higher tier answers fuller, but they contain a greater variety of tenses and a greater number of personal opinions with a good justification.

2
Rôle-play A *(page 76)*

Lehrer(in): Du bist mit deinem Brieffreund in Deutschland. Ihr sprecht über das Wochenende. Dein Brieffreund beginnt.

Wollen wir am Samstag ins Kino gehen?

Du: **Ja, gerne. Was läuft am Samstagabend?**ᵃ

Lehrer(in): Möchtest du den neuen James-Bond-Film sehen?

Du: **Ja, gute Idee, weil ich diesen Film noch nicht gesehen habe.**ᵇ **James-Bond-Filme gefallen mir sehr gut.**ᶜ

> **a** You could also say *Welchen Film gibt es im Kino?*, but *Was läuft?* is a good and often used expression.
>
> **b** This is an unprepared question, so of course, you may have seen this film already. In that case you would say *Nein, danke, weil ich diesen Film schon gesehen habe.*
>
> **c** If you are not very confident with *weil*, you can still give a reason by simply starting a new sentence to explain. The verb *gefallen* is impressive and you could say *Nein, danke. James-Bond-Filme gefallen mir überhaupt nicht.*

Lehrer(in): O.K. Was möchtest du am Sonntag machen?

Du: Können wir schwimmen gehen?^d

Lehrer(in): In Ordnung. Wann stehst du normalerweise am Sonntag auf?

Du: Gegen neun oder halb zehn.^e

Lehrer(in): Mm… Was machst du mit deinen Freunden in Wales am Wochenende?

Du: Ich gehe in die Stadt und treffe mich mit meinen Freunden im Eiscafé.^f

d You have a free choice of activities. How about *Ich möchte eine Wanderung machen; Könnten wir Radfahren?; Wie wär's mit einer Bootsfahrt auf dem See?*

e It's a good answer with *gegen* (about) giving two different times and especially using *halb* correctly.

f Again you have a free hand here, but keep it fairly brief in a rôle-play. You could say *Am Samstag habe ich Netzballtraining und dann meine Klavierstunde. Sonntag ist besser, ich bin frei und treffe mich normalerweise mit meinen Freunden, um Kaffee/ Cola/Tee zu trinken oder im Park/in der Stadt zu bummeln.*

Rôle-play B *(page 77)*

Lehrer(in): Du bist bei deiner Austauschpartnerin zu Besuch. Ich bin deine Austauschpartnerin.

Wir gehen ins Sportzentrum.

Du: Um wieviel Uhr gehen wir?

Lehrer(in): Um zehn Uhr. Was für Sport treibst du gern?

Du: Ich spiele sehr gern Tennis und schwimme jede Woche.

Lehrer(in): Klasse! Ich auch.

Du: Fahren wir mit dem Bus dorthin?

Lehrer(in): Nein, es ist nicht weit. Wir gehen zu Fuß.

Du: Kann man dort etwas essen?

Lehrer(in): Ja, natürlich.

These responses are the ones expected by the ULEAC examiner, except where the words are underlined, and they allow 'any suitable sport' or 'other appropriate transport'. You can see that a straightforward answer is all that is required. You can save your longer answers for the conversation afterwards.

Many rôle-play parts, like these ones, are questions. You need to make sure you know all your question words really well and remember about turning the verb and subject around to form a question. Learn some examples, such as those above, to serve as models.

Conversation A *(page 77)*

1 Wenn du keine Schulaufgaben hast, was machst du gern?

   Ich spiele gern Gitarre und ich treibe gern Sport. Ich bin Mitglied in einem Sportverein.

2 Wieviel Taschengeld bekommst du?

   Ich bekomme fünf Pfund pro Woche.

3 Wofür gibst du dein Taschengeld aus?

   Ich kaufe mir Kassetten und Süßigkeiten. Letztes Wochenende habe ich mir ein tolles T-Shirt gekauft.

4 Sparst du dein Geld?

   Ich möchte sehr gerne sparen, aber ich kann es nicht, weil ich nicht genug Geld kriege.

5 Hast du einen Job, um Geld zu verdienen?

   Nein, aber ich möchte in einem Café oder in einem Restaurant arbeiten. Es ist sehr schwer, es gibt so wenig Jobs in meiner Stadt.

Conversation B *(page 78)*

1 Was hast du letztes Wochenende gemacht?

Letztes Wochenende war es sehr langweilig. Ich mußte die ganze Zeit arbeiten, weil ich diese Examen habe. Ich bin das ganze Wochenende in meinem Zimmer geblieben, um mich auf die Examen vorzubereiten.

2 Was hast du nach den Examen vor?

Ich möchte nach Deutschland fahren, aber das ist leider nicht möglich, weil ich im Juli ein Betriebspraktikum machen muß.

3 Wo verbringst du deine Sommerferien dieses Jahr?

Im August fahre ich nach Schottland mit meinen Eltern, das wird toll! Ich fahre sehr gern in die schottischen Berge, um zu wandern oder zu angeln.

4 Mit wem gehst du gern aus?

Ich gehe natürlich am liebsten mit meinen Freunden aus, denn wir haben Spaß zusammen. Letztes Wochenende, zum Beispiel, bin ich mit ihnen zum Sportzentrum gegangen. Das Fußballspiel war prima – wir waren die Sieger!

Conversation C *(page 78)*

1 Wenn du nach Deutschland fahren könntest, was möchtest du da machen?

Ich möchte die Stadt besuchen, wo meine Brieffreundin wohnt. Dann könnte ich ihre Freunde kennenlernen. Das wäre fabelhaft!

2 Was machst du am liebsten in deiner Freizeit?

Ich fahre sehr gerne Rad. Ich habe ein tolles Mountainbike und fahre oft aufs Land oder in den Wald. Leider konnte ich letztes Wochenende nicht radfahren, weil ich mich auf dieses Examen vorbereiten mußte. In den Sommerferien werde ich aber jeden Tag eine Radtour machen. Ich freue mich sehr darauf!

3 Bekommst du deiner Meinung nach genug Taschengeld?

Ja, Radfahren ist ziemlich billig als Hobby, aber ab und zu muß ich etwas reparieren, und das kann ziemlich teuer sein. Deshalb trage ich jeden Abend Zeitungen aus. Mit dem Geld und dem, was meine Eltern mir geben, habe ich genug.

4 Erzähl mir von einem Film, den du neulich gesehen hast.

Ich habe den Titel vergessen, aber es handelt sich um einen jungen Mann, dessen Freund an einer Drogenüberdosis starb. Er wollte irgendwie den Drogenhändler finden, aber es wurde schrecklich gefährlich, und er mußte einen Privatdetektiv einsetzen. Es war eine Detektivin, und die zwei verliebten sich, als sie zusammen gegen die Drogenbande kämpften. Was ich unheimlich gut gefunden habe, waren die spannende Geschichte und die guten Schauspieler. Der Film war wirklich prima, es lohnt sich, ihn zu sehen.

3
Rôle-play A *(page 79)*

Lehrer(in): Also, wir sind in Deutschland, ich bin dein(e) Freund(in). So... was wolltest du fragen?

> **Du: Könnten wir einen Abend ausgehen?**

Lehrer(in): Wollen wir ins Kino gehen?

> **Du: Ja, das wäre schön. Ich bin am Mittwoch oder Donnerstag frei – geht das?**

Lehrer(in): Nein, Mittwoch und Donnerstag kann ich nicht – ich habe zu viele Hausaufgaben zu machen.

> **Du: Ach, schade. Montag gehe ich schwimmen, und am Freitag ist die Disco.**

Lehrer(in): Mußt du unbedingt schwimmen gehen?

> **Du: Ja, ich habe es meinem Freund versprochen. Wir wollen ins Wellenbad, aber wir gehen um fünf Uhr.**

Lehrer(in): Wir können also zu der Spätvorstellung um halb elf gehen.

> **Du: Gute Idee! Dann treffen wir uns vor dem Kino um Viertel nach zehn.**

This model is one of many variations and you and the teacher have to interact very carefully, each responding to the other's questions or comments. You could, for example, decide to cancel the swimming on Monday and say Nein, das ist mir egal. Ich kann in England schwimmen gehen. Ich möchte einen deutschen Film sehen. Ich rufe meinen Freund an.

Rôle-play B *(page 79)*

Lehrer(in): Du rufst eine Freundin an. Ich bin die Freundin.
Hallo, Bauer.

> **Du: Hallo, hier spricht Emily.**

Lehrer(in): Ach, hallo Emily, wie geht's?

> **Du: Gut, danke.**

Lehrer(in): Was machen wir morgen?

> **Du: Ich habe einen Vorschlag. Wollen wir zum Freizeitzentrum gehen? Wir könnten den ganzen Tag bleiben. Es gibt ein Freibad, viele Spiele und einen Schnellimbiß.**

Lehrer(in): Sollen wir etwas zu essen mitnehmen?

> **Du: Nein, es macht Spaß, Würstchen und Pommes frites zu kaufen.**

Lehrer(in): Wann und wo treffen wir uns?

> **Du: Um zehn Uhr vor dem Zentrum. Geht das?**

Lehrer(in): Ja. Wer kommt noch mit?

> **Du: Meine Brieffreundin und ihre Schwester möchten auch mitkommen, wenn du nichts dagegen hast.**

Lehrer(in): Nein. Was machen wir, wenn es regnet?

> **Du: Ach, dem Wetterbericht nach ist es sonnig und warm morgen.**

Lehrer(in): Gut. Wie lange gehen wir?

> **Du: Von zehn bis neunzehn Uhr.**

Lehrer(in): Also, bis dann, Wiederhören.

Learn some useful phrases from this rôle-play and remember that you can often use these kinds of expressions in your writing exam as well: **Ich habe einen Vorschlag** *(I've a suggestion);* **es macht Spaß ... zu ...** *(It's fun to . . .);* **von zehn bis neunzehn Uhr** *(from ten 'til seven o'clock)*.

Solutions
Speaking

4
Rôle-play A *(page 83)*

Lehrer(in): Du bist in einem Café. Ich bin dein deutscher Freund. Das war eine tolle Party gestern abend, nicht wahr?

Du: Ja, sehr gut. Was machst du heute abend?

Lehrer(in): Ich weiß nicht.

Du: Wollen wir ins Kino gehen?ᵃ

Lehrer(in): Ja, gute Idee. Ich habe die Zeitung hier. Laß uns gucken.

Du: Um wieviel Uhr beginnt die letzte Vorstellung?ᵇ

Lehrer(in): Es gibt einen guten Krimi um halb neun.

Du: Prima. Also, bis heute abend – tschüs!ᶜ

Lehrer(in): Gut. Bis später.

a You could also say *Möchtest du ins Kino gehen?* (Would you like to go to the cinema?)

b A simpler version such as *Wann beginnt der Film?* will also gain full marks. Use whatever you are most confident with. It's worth noting alternative versions, because you might hear them in a listening test!

c *Auf Wiedersehen* would be enough here, but you could add *Bis später* (See you later) if you wish. The less formal *Tschüs* (Bye!) is perfectly acceptable for speaking to your friend. Learn your responses by heart, if you're not sure of any of them.

Rôle-play B *(page 83)*

Lehrer(in): Hallo, hier spricht Stefanie. Kann ich John sprechen?

Du: Hallo, John am Apparat. Sag mal, Stefanie, wollen wir heute abend ins Kino gehen?ᵃ

Lehrer(in): Oh, ich weiß nicht. Ich gehe lieber kegeln. Die ganze Bande geht heute abend zur Kegelbahn.

Du: Ach, das ist nicht für mich. Außerdem wollte ich mit dir alleine ausgehen.ᵇ

Lehrer(in): O.K. Dann gehe ich mit dir aus.

Du: Was läuft heute im Kino, weißt du das?

Lehrer(in): Also, im Kapitol laufen ein Krimi, eine Komödie, und ein Horrorfilm. Was meinst du?

Du: Ich sehe lieber die Komödie. Das macht Spaß, und die anderen sind meistens ganz einfach dumm.ᶜ

Lehrer(in): Einverstanden, ich habe sowieso diesen Film mit Schwarzenegger gesehen.

Du: Wann und wo treffen wir uns?

Lehrer(in): Ich nehme Vatis Auto. Ich hole dich um acht ab.

Du: Toll. Ich freue mich darauf. Wiederhören.ᵈ

Lehrer(in): Wiederhören.

In Higher tier rôle-plays especially, you need to be prepared to 'play' your part. You have to pretend the conversation is real and bring in as many realistic ideas as you can. The teacher has a good idea of what you need to say to get the marks in that particular rôle and you should follow the cues you are given very closely.

a You can choose when to go out so you could use *am Wochenende, am Freitag, nächste Woche*.

b This has to be a speedy response to an unprepared question and there are many alternatives: *Ich kann nicht kegeln, Ich habe mich an der Hand verletzt.* (I can't bowl, my hand is injured); *Ich kegle nicht gern. Ich bin total ungeschickt.* (I don't like bowling. I'm really clumsy.); *Ich war gestern schon kegeln. Ich wollte wirklich ins Kino gehen.* (I went bowling yesterday. I really wanted to go to the cinema.)

c The choice of film is up to you, as is the reason. Try also: *Ich mag Komödien nicht und Horrorfilme sind langweilig. Ein guter Krimi ist immer spannend.* (I don't like comedies and horror films are boring. A good thriller is always exciting.)

d Don't forget you are on the telephone – *Wiederhören.* (Literally – hear you again. Learn the phrase: *Ich freue mich darauf* (I'm looking forward to it.). You can often use it in writing too – *Ich freue mich auf meinen Aufenthalt in Deutschland.* (I'm looking forward to my stay in Germany.)

Area C

1
Conversation A *(page 84)*

1 Beschreib die Stadt, in der du wohnst.

   Ich wohne in York, im Norden von England.ᵃ Die Stadt ist schön und interessant. Es gibt eine alte Burg, einen großen Dom und interessante Museen.ᵇ Ich wohne sehr gern hier.ᶜ

2 Und was gibt es dort für Teenager?

   Es ist viel los: Wir haben ein Kino und ein Hallenbad.ᵈ Letztes Wochenende, zum Beispiel, war ich in der Disco – das war toll!ᵉ Nächste Woche gehe ich ins Theater, auch das gefällt mir sehr!

3 Wie kommst du von deinem Haus zur Stadtmitte? Fährst du mit dem Bus, oder?

   Normalerweise gehe ich zu Fuß. Wenn es regnet, nehme ich den Bus.ᶠ Letzte Woche bin ich zweimal mit dem Rad gefahren.ᵍ

4 Und wie ist das Wetter dort im Winter?

   Meistens ist es ziemlich kalt und regnerisch, aber letztes Jahr hat es viel geschneit und gefroren.ʰ

5 Also, wohnst du gern dort?

   Ja, weil die Stadt sehr schön ist, und ich dort viele Freunde habe.ⁱ Und Sie, wohnen Sie gern in Ihrer Stadt?ʲ

a Learn to say where your town is: *Ich wohne in … im Norden/im Süden/im Westen/im Osten/im Nordosten/im Südwesten von England/Schottland/Wales/Irland/Nordirland.*

b This sentence has enough information and adjectives to score well – adapt it to describe your own town.

c It's good to express an opinion here. You may prefer to say *Ich wohne nicht gern hier.*

d Learn to say what you can do in your town, e.g. *Es gibt ein tolles Sportzentrum. Man kann im Stadion guten Fußball sehen.*

e Excellent for gaining marks – a reference to the past followed by a reference to the future. *Letzte Woche* and *nächste Woche* are simple ways into such sentences. Once again an opinion, this time using *Das gefällt mir sehr.* (I really enjoy that.)

f You can adapt this to your own travelling arrangements, using phrases such as *mit dem Auto; mit dem Zug …* or changing the weather, e.g. *Wenn das Wetter schön ist, …*

g Another good past tense and good use of *zweimal* (twice).

h Top marks for two kinds of weather and the impressive use of two weather verbs in the past tense.

i Very good use of *weil* with the two verbs sent to the end of their clause, to give a good opinion.

j It is good to finish this answer with a question to the teacher. She or he will only answer briefly but it makes it more like a real conversation and not an interrogation!

Conversation B *(page 84)*

1 Seit wann wohnst du dort?

   Ich wohne seit zehn Jahren in Leeds. Vorher wohnten wir in Folkestone in Südengland.ᵃ Ich bin lieber in Leeds, weil die Stadt viel interessanter ist. In Folkestone gibt es zu viele Touristen.ᵇ

2 Wenn du viel Geld hättest, wo würdest du gerne wohnen?

   Das ist eine schwere Frage.ᶜ Ich würde in Leeds bleiben, aber in einen reichen Vorort umziehen. Viele Leute würden aufs Land ziehen, aber ich bleibe lieber in der Nähe einer Großstadt, weil dort viel mehr los ist.ᵈ

a This is an excellent reply to learn, using the simple past of *wohnen* with *vorher* (previously).

b Just what the examiner hopes to hear – an opinion backed up by a *weil* justification. The last part is the icing on the cake!

c A useful way to get yourself time to think and work out your answer. You could also say, *Ich weiß nicht genau, aber…* (I don't know exactly, but…)

d This reply has many excellent features – two uses of *würde(n)* (would), an opinion expressed by *lieber* (rather) and a good justification with a *weil*-clause.

Solutions
Speaking

3 Was sollte man in deiner Stadt für die Jugendlichen tun?

   Es gibt schon viele Freizeitangebote für Erwachsene. Für Jugendliche gibt es noch zu wenig.[e] Man könnte zum Beispiel einen Freizeitpark oder eine Eishalle bauen und das alte Hallenbad renovieren.[f]

4 Beschreib eine Stadt oder eine Gegend in Deutschland.

   Leider bin ich noch nie in Deutschland gewesen, aber ich habe schon viel über Köln gehört und gelesen.[g] Das ist, sagt man, eine sehr lebendige Stadt. Dort kann man den Kölner Dom und viele interessante Museen besichtigen. Ich interessiere mich sehr für Musik, und in Köln findet man ein großes Musikangebot. Zum Beispiel Konzerte für Klassik, Pop und Jazz. Ich würde sehr gerne dort Urlaub machen.[h]

5 Weißt du die Wettervorhersage für morgen?

   Es soll den ganzen Tag regnen und für die Jahreszeit zu kalt und sehr windig sein. Das ist schade, nicht wahr?[i] Ich wollte morgen wandern gehen, aber bei so einem Wetter macht das keinen Spaß.[j]

[e] You may want to start more positively if you have good leisure opportunities in your town: *Für Jugendliche gibt es schon viele Freizeitangebote – zum Beispiel das Sportzentrum, viele Discos und zwei Kinos, aber ...* (For young people there are already many free time opportunities – for example the sports centre, many discos and two cinemas ...)

[f] This is a good point-scoring sentence, using *man könnte* (they could) with both second verbs sent to the end and three suggestions.

[g] Two references to the past and three past tense verbs!

[h] You can adapt this to your own interests, but make a point of learning something about one or two well-known towns or regions in German-speaking countries. Most of them could be described as: ... *... ist eine schöne, interessante Stadt/Gegend, wo viel los ist.* (... is a lovely, interesting town where a lot is happening.)

[i] A good opinion formed by a question.

[j] *Ich wollte ...* (I wanted to . . .) is a good way to refer to the past and here it brings in another opinion.

2
Rôle-play A *(page 86)*

Lehrer(in): Sie sind in Deutschland. Ich bin ein Passant.

              Guten Tag.

Du: Entschuldigen Sie, bitte. Wo ist der Bahnhof?[a]

Lehrer(in): Gehen Sie geradeaus bis zum Krankenhaus. Dort gehen Sie links.

Du: Ist es weit von hier?[b]

Lehrer(in): Ja, ziemlich weit – vier Kilometer.

Du: Gibt es einen Bus zum Bahnhof?[c]

Lehrer(in): Ja, Linie 12.

Du: Danke schön.

Lehrer(in): Bitte schön.

[a] This is an essential question and this is the simplest form for asking the way. You could use the question *Wie komme ich am besten zum Bahnhof, bitte?* (What is the best way to the station, please?). Remember to change the *zum* to *zur* if you are asking the way to a place which is a feminine noun, e.g. *Wie komme ich am besten zur Fußgängerzone?* (What is the best way to the pedestrian area?).

[b] An alternative question is *Ist es weit entfernt?* (Is it far away?)

[c] You can adapt this to ask about other means of transport, e.g. *Gibt es einen Zug/ein Flugzeug/eine Straßenbahn?* (Is there a train/plane/tram?). A more impressive form would be *Kann man mit dem Bus dahin fahren?* (Can you get there by bus?).

Rôle-play B *(page 86)*

Lehrer(in): Sie sind in der Stadt. Ich bin eine Touristin.

              Entschuldigung. Ist hier in der Nähe eine Post?

Du: Ja, gehen Sie hier geradeaus und über die Brücke.[a]

Lehrer(in): Gut, geradeaus und über die Brücke ...

Du: Und dann nehmen Sie die zweite Straße links.[a]

[a] Try making up variations of these directions, e.g. *Gehen Sie bis zur Kreuzung ... Sie gehen an der Post vorbei ... Sie gehen hier rechts ...* (Go to the crossroads ... Go past the post office ... Turn right here ...)

Solutions
Speaking

Lehrer(in): Und ist es weit von hier?

Du: Oh ja, drei Kilometer.[b]

Lehrer(in): Danke. Können Sie mir bitte sagen, ob die Post offen ist?

Du: Ja, bis fünf Uhr.[c]

Lehrer(in): Vielen Dank.

[b] Other ways of saying how far away somewhere is may involve time and the means of getting there, e.g. *Es ist fünf Minuten zu Fuß./Es ist zehn Minuten mit dem Auto.* (It's five minutes on foot./It's ten minutes by car.)

[c] Don't forget how important numbers are and how often the time comes up in every part of your exam. Revise using phrases such as: *Bis Viertel nach sechs./Bis Mitternacht./Bis neun Uhr fünfundvierzig.* (Until quarter past six./Until midnight./Until 9.45.)

3
Rôle-play A *(page 87)*

Lehrer(in): Sie kaufen Andenken. Ich bin die Verkäuferin.

Guten Tag.

Du: Guten Tag.

Lehrer(in): Kann ich Ihnen helfen?

Du: Ich möchte eine Schachtel Pralinen und das Buch hier, bitte.[a]

Lehrer(in): Ja, gut.

Du: Was kostet das, bitte?[b]

Lehrer(in): DM 4,50.

Du: Danke schön.

Lehrer(in): Bitte schön.

Du: Auf Wiedersehen.

Lehrer(in): Auf Wiedersehen.

[a] You could also ask for *Ein Paar Socken* (A pair of socks.); *Einen Füller* (A fountain pen.); *Ein T-Shirt* (A T-shirt.); *Eine Flasche Parfüm* (A bottle of perfume.)

[b] Another way to ask the cost is to say *Was macht das zusammen, bitte?* (What's that all together, please?)

Rôle-play B *(page 87)*

Lehrer(in): Sie sind auf dem Campingplatz im Geschäft. Ich bin der Verkäufer.

Bitte schön?

Du: Geben Sie mir bitte vier Brötchen und zwei Scheiben Schinken.[a]

Lehrer(in): Sonst noch etwas?

Du: Ja, ich möchte ein Pfund Äpfel.[b]

Lehrer(in): Bitte schön.

Du: Haben Sie eine große Flasche Cola?

Lehrer(in): Das habe ich heute leider nicht.

Du: Ach schade. Also, eine Flasche Limonade, bitte.[c]

Lehrer(in): O.K. Das macht DM 12,75 zusammen. Wie lange bleiben Sie hier?

Du: Bitte schön. Nur noch zwei Tage, leider.[d]

Lehrer(in): Danke schön. Viel Spaß!

[a] You could also say here *Ein halbes Pfund Käse und ein Vollkornbrot, bitte.* (Half a pound of cheese and a wholemeal loaf, please.)

[b] The choice of fruit and the quantity are yours again: *Ein Kilo Bananen/zwei Pfirsiche/fünfhundert Gramm Kirschen/ein Körbchen Erdbeeren.* (Two pounds or a kilo of bananas/two peaches/500 grams of cherries/a punnet of strawberries)

[c] A good response to an unpredictable reply. You could say *Das macht nichts.* (It doesn't matter.)

[d] You could also say *Noch eine Woche* (Another week) or *Wir fahren morgen weiter.* (We're moving on tomorrow.)

Solutions
Speaking

Rôle-play C *(page 87)*

Lehrer(in): Sie sind in einem Geschenkladen. Ich bin die Verkäuferin.

Du: **Entschuldigung, ich habe dieses T-Shirt für meinen Bruder gekauft, aber es hat ein kleines Loch hier, sehen Sie?ᵃ**

Lehrer(in): Wann haben Sie das gekauft?

Du: **Heute vormittag. Gegen halb elf.ᵇ**

Lehrer(in): Ja, Sie haben recht. Das geht nicht. Es tut mir sehr leid. Was wollen Sie machen?

Du: **Können Sie es umtauschen?ᶜ**

Lehrer(in): Leider haben wir das nicht mehr in dieser Farbe.

Du: **Könnte ich vielleicht etwas Anderes wählen?ᵈ**

Lehrer(in): Ja, sicher. Das ist kein Problem.

a There are many possibilities here, e.g. *Ich habe eine kleine Puppe/ein Taschenmesser/eine Lampe für meine Mutter/für meine Schwester/für meinen Vater gekauft, aber sie/es ist kaputt.* (I bought a little doll/a penknife/a torch for my mother/for my sister/for my father, but it's broken.)

b A good chance to show off your knowledge of times. *Gegen* (About) is good.

c You can decide here; perhaps *Haben Sie ein Anderes?* (Have you another one?)

d You may want to be less co-operative and ask for your money back. *Dann möchte ich mein Geld zurück, bitte.*

4
Rôle-play A *(page 88)*

Lehrer(in): Sie sind auf der Post. Ich bin der Angestellte.

Kann ich Ihnen helfen?

Du: **Was kostet eine Postkarte nach England, bitte?ᵃ**

Lehrer(in): Nach England, achtzig Pfennig.

Du: **Drei Briefmarken zu achtzig Pfennig, bitte.**

Lehrer(in): DM 2,40, bitte.

Du: **Es tut mir leid. Ich habe nur einen Fünfzigmarkschein.ᵇ**

Lehrer(in): Kein Problem, bitte schön.

Du: **Danke schön. Auf Wiedersehen.**

Lehrer(in): Auf Wiedersehen.

a This sentence can easily be adapted, e.g. *Was kostet ein Brief nach Frankreich?* (How much is a letter to France?)

b You could say *Können Sie einen Fünfzigmarkschein wechseln?* (Can you change a fifty mark note?) or even *Ich habe kein Kleingeld, hier sind fünfzig Mark.* (I've no change, here are 50 marks.)

Rôle-play B *(page 88)*

Lehrer(in): Sie gehen in eine Bank in Deutschland. Sie haben kein deutsches Geld mehr, aber Sie haben Reiseschecks. Ich bin der Angestellte.

Guten Tag. Kann ich Ihnen helfen?

Du: **Ich möchte diese Reiseschecks einlösen, bitte.ᵃ**

Lehrer(in): Wie viele und was für Reiseschecks haben Sie?

Du: **Ich habe zwei zu zwanzig Pfund.**

Lehrer(in): Wo wohnen Sie hier in Deutschland?

Du: **Ich wohne bei meinem Brieffreund.ᵇ**

Lehrer(in): Darf ich Ihren Paß haben?

Du: **Ich habe meinen Paß nicht. Er ist in meinem Schlafzimmer.ᶜ**

a Learn this useful sentence. It can be varied using *wechseln* (to change) instead of *einlösen*.

b You are free here to say any place, so choose somewhere you know, e.g. *Ich bin auf dem Campingplatz/in der Jugendherberge/in einem Hotel.* (I'm on the campsite/in the youth hostel/in an hotel.)

c Again you can say anything you can manage, e.g. *Ich habe ihn vergessen/verloren.* (I've forgotten/lost it.) *Er ist zu Hause/im Auto/im Wohnwagen/im Zelt.* (It's at home/in the car/in the caravan/in the tent.) here are 50 marks.)

Lehrer(in): Es tut mir leid, aber Sie müssen mit dem Paß zurückkommen.

Du: Bis wieviel Uhr sind Sie offen?

Lehrer(in): Heute bis achtzen Uhr.

Rôle-play C *(page 89)*

Lehrer(in): Sie sind im Fundbüro in Deutschland. Ich bin die Angestellte. Guten Tag. Was kann ich für Sie tun?

Du: Ich habe meinen Fotoapparat verloren.

Lehrer(in): Wo haben Sie ihn verloren, meinen Sie?

Du: Ich weiß nicht genau.[a] Vielleicht im Einkaufszentrum.

Lehrer(in): Um wieviel Uhr war das?

Du: Heute vormittag, zwischen halb neun und elf Uhr.[b]

Lehrer(in): Und können Sie den Apparat beschreiben?

Du: Er ist ziemlich klein, schwarz, automatisch, hat einen eingebauten Blitz und ist in einer dunkelgrünen Tasche.[c]

Lehrer(in): Ja, wir müssen dieses Formular ausfüllen. Welcher Name, bitte?

Du: Spedding.

Lehrer(in): Und wie schreibt man das?

Du: S-P-E-D-D-I-N-G. [d]

Lehrer(in): Danke. Warten Sie bitte einen Moment.

[a] This sentence adds realism to the conversation, as does the *vielleicht* (perhaps).

[b] Again a chance to show off some more complicated times rather than simply saying *Um neun Uhr*!

[c] You can really go into detail describing lost property, but it is safer to stick to two or three details and to use mainly words you know.

[d] Don't forget to practise your German alphabet – it can crop up anywhere!

Rôle-play A *(page 89)*

Lehrer(in): Sie wollen mit dem Zug fahren. Ich bin der Fahrkartenverkäufer. Bitte schön?

Du: Gibt es einen Zug von hier nach Bonn?[a]

Lehrer(in): Wann wollen Sie fahren?

Du: Am Montag.[b]

Lehrer(in): Um wieviel Uhr?

Du: Gegen sechzehn Uhr.

Lehrer(in): O.K. Es gibt einen Zug um 16.20 Uhr.

Du: Also, einmal nach Bonn, bitte.[c]

Lehrer(in): Also, das macht DM 15.

Du: Muß ich umsteigen?[d]

Lehrer(in): Nein, der Zug fährt direkt.

[a] You can adapt this sentence to other situations: *Gibt es einen Flug nach Genf?* (Is there a flight to Geneva?); *Gibt es einen Bus nach Wien?* (Is there a bus to Vienna?) Another common variation involves asking the time of departure: *Wann fährt der Zug/der Bus/das Schiff nach Zürich/München/Boppard?* (What time is the train/bus/boat/to Zürich/Munich/Boppard?)

[b] Make sure you know all the days of the week: *Montag, Dienstag, Mittwoch, Donnerstag, Freitag, Samstag (oder Sonnabend), Sonntag.*

[c] You could have asked *Einmal nach Bonn, hin und zürück, bitte.* (A return ticket to Bonn, please.)

[d] An alternative way to find this out is to ask: *Fährt der Zug direkt?* (Is it a direct train?)

Solutions
Speaking

Rôle-play B *(page 90)*

Lehrer(in): Sie sind am Bahnhof. Ich bin die Beamtin.

Bitte schön?

Du: **Ich möchte eine Rückfahrkarte nach Bonn, bitte.**[a]

Lehrer(in): Wann fahren Sie?

Du: **Nächsten Montag.**

Lehrer(in): Ja, das geht.

Du: **Muß ich reservieren?**[b]

Lehrer(in): Nein, das macht DM 63.

Du: **Wo sind die Toiletten, bitte?**[c]

Lehrer(in): Rechts neben dem Zeitungskiosk.

[a] You have a choice here, so pick the one you are certain of. You could also say: *Einmal nach Bonn einfach, bitte.* (A single ticket to Bonn, please.)

[b] You could also ask: *Kann ich einen Platz reservieren, bitte?* (Can I reserve a seat, please?)

[c] The picture stimulus also gives you the choice of: *Wo ist das Restaurant/ der Schnellimbiß?* (Where is the restaurant/snack-bar?) or *Wo ist das Informationsbüro?* (Where is the information office?).

Rôle-play C *(page 90)*

Lehrer(in): Wir sind an einer Tankstelle. Ich bin der Tankwart.

Guten Tag. Kann ich Ihnen helfen?

Du: **Ja, Bleifrei, bitte.**[a]

Lehrer(in): Ja, wieviel möchten Sie?

Du: **Für fünfzig Mark, bitte.**[b]

Lehrer(in): Bitte schön. Sonst noch etwas?

Du: **Ja, könnten Sie die Reifen prüfen?**[c]

Lehrer(in): Ach, es tut mir leid. Die Pumpe ist kaputt.

Du: **Oh, schade. Das ist dumm. Wo ist die nächste Tankstelle?**

Lehrer(in): Also, es gibt eine andere Tankstelle ungefähr sieben Kilometer von hier.

Du: **Danke. Und wo sind die Toiletten, bitte?**

Lehrer(in): Es tut mir leid, aber die Toiletten sind im Moment geschlossen zum Putzen.

Du: **Wann werden sie fertig sein?**[d]

Lehrer(in): Oh, in fünf oder zehn Minuten.

[a] Here you could ask for other sorts of fuel: *Normal/Super/Diesel.*

[b] Other answers include: *Volltanken, bitte.* (Fill it up, please.); *Fünfzig Liter, bitte.* (Fifty litres, please.); *Zwanzig Liter, bitte.* (Twenty litres, please.)

[c] You may also have been required to ask the attendant: *Könnten Sie das Öl/das Wasser prüfen, bitte?* (Could you check the oil/water, please?).

[d] Another good reaction here would have been: *Gibt es andere Toiletten in der Nähe?* (Are there other toilets nearby?)

Area D

2
Conversation A *(page 93)* and B *(page 94)*

1 The first three opinions <u>which are justified</u> are:

– **Nicht sehr viel. Ich bekomme nur drei Pfund die Stunde.**
– **Nein, nicht besonders. Es ist langweilig und die Kunden sind manchmal gemein.**

- Also, der Vorteil ist natürlich das Geld, weil ich mit meinen Freunden in Urlaub fahren kann. Der größte Nachteil ist, daß mein ganzes Wochenende nur aus Arbeit besteht, und ich keine Zeit habe auszugehen.

2 Here are the first three references to the past:

- Also, normalerweise arbeite ich samstags und sonntags, aber letztes Wochenende habe ich nicht gearbeitet, weil ich diese Prüfung vorbereiten mußte.
- Meine Eltern kaufen dort ein und haben ein Stellenangebot im Geschäft gesehen.
- Seit einem Jahr. Ich habe letzten Juli angefangen.

3 These are the first three references to the present:

- Ja, ich arbeite, weil ich Geld zum Ausgeben brauche.
- Das macht auch Spaß.
- Ich arbeite im Supermarkt am Stadtrand.

4 The first three references to the future are:

- Ich spare für die Ferien. Ich fahre dieses Jahr mit meinen Freunden nach Spanien in Urlaub.
- Ich hoffe, nach den Examen etwas Besseres zu finden.
- Ja, ich möchte in Deutschland arbeiten. Vielleicht könnte ich das Jahr, bevor ich an die Uni gehe, in Berlin verbringen.

Rôle-play A *(page 95)*

Lehrer(in): Wir sind in Deutschland. Ich bin die Mutter von deinem Brieffreund.

Wann beginnt die Arbeit am Montag?

Du: Um halb neun.[a]

Lehrer(in): Wie fährst du zur Arbeit?

Du: Mit dem Bus.[a]

Lehrer(in): Wie lange dauert dein Praktikum?

Du: Zwei Wochen.[b]

Lehrer(in): Welchen Job hast du in England?

Du: Ich trage Zeitungen aus.[c]

[a] For both these responses you need only use a phrase to gain full marks, but equally correct would be *Die Arbeit beginnt um halb neun/acht Uhr dreißig* and *Ich fahre mit dem Bus*.

[b] You could also say *Vierzehn Tage*.

[c] Another useful way to say this is *Ich bin Zeitungsjunge/Zeitungsmädchen*.

Rôle-play B *(page 96)*

Lehrer(in): Sie wollen in einem Restaurant in Freiburg arbeiten. Sie gehen zu einem Restaurant, in dem man Arbeitskräfte braucht.

Guten Tag. Kann ich Ihnen helfen?

Du: Ich heiße Marion Johnson.[a] **Ich suche einen Job als Kellnerin.**[b]

Lehrer(in): Ach so. Wie alt sind Sie, und was ist Ihre Nationalität?

Du: Ich bin sechzehn Jahre alt. Ich komme aus England.[c]

[a] Always be ready to spell your name or address whenever you are asked for them. You can check the pronunciation of the German alphabet in *GCSE German Vocabulary*.

[b] You might also have said, *Ich möchte im Restaurant arbeiten. Brauchen Sie Hilfe?* (I'd like to work in the restaurant. Do you need help?)

[c] Another way to give your nationality is to say *Ich bin Engländer(in)/Schottin/Waliser(in)/Ire(Irin)* (I'm an Englishman(woman)/a Scot/a Welshman(woman)/an Irishman(woman).)

Solutions
Speaking

Lehrer(in): Haben Sie Arbeitserfahrung in einem Restaurant?

Du: Ja, ich arbeite seit anderthalb Jahren als Kellnerin in einem guten Restaurant in York.[d]

Lehrer(in): Wie lange werden Sie in Freiburg bleiben?

Du: Ich möchte zwei Monate hier in Freiburg bleiben.

Lehrer(in): Gut. Wann können Sie anfangen zu arbeiten?

Du: Ich könnte sofort anfangen, oder morgen früh, wenn Sie wollen.[e]

[d] This is a good answer because it uses *seit* (for) with the correct tense (present) and also the word *anderthalb* (one and a half). Notice too, the adjective describing the restaurant.

[e] Again a full answer, which will impress the examiner more than simply saying a day of the week.

Rôle-play C *(page 96)*

Lehrer(in): Sie rufen beim Jugendklub an. Ich bin Frau Krüger.

Hallo. Krüger.

Du: Guten Tag, Frau Krüger.

Lehrer(in): Wie kann ich Ihnen helfen?

Du: Ich möchte in dem Jugendklub aushelfen.

Lehrer(in): Erzählen Sie mir etwas über sich. Wie heißen Sie? Wie alt sind Sie?

Du: Ich heiße James Morgan. Ich bin sechzehn Jahre alt. Ich bin Engländer.

Lehrer(in): Haben Sie schon mal in einem Jugendklub gearbeitet?

Du: Nein, leider nicht. Aber ich habe mein Betriebspraktikum in einer Grundschule gemacht. Die Schüler waren zehn oder elf Jahre alt. Es hat viel Spaß gemacht, weil wir viele verschiedene Aktivitäten gemacht haben, und die Schüler sehr lebhaft waren.[a]

Lehrer(in): Gut. Wann könnten Sie anfangen?

Du: Heute, wenn Sie wollen.

Lehrer(in): Wie oft könnten Sie kommen?

Du: Drei- oder viermal in der Woche, oder öfter, wenn es nötig wäre.[b]

Lehrer(in): Sehr gut. Also, wo sind Sie tagsüber zu erreichen?

Du: Ich wohne bei einer deutschen Familie hier in der Nähe. Familie Schnapp, Drosselweg 45. Die Telefonnummer ist 24 67 37 75.[c]

Lehrer(in): Vielen Dank. Ich rufe Sie heute abend an. Auf Wiederhören.

[a] This is an excellent, full answer, which cleverly brings in two different past tenses and a well-justified opinion, which, as you know, are good for collecting high marks. Notice too, that it is of the *Nein, aber ...* type, so that no opportunity to impress is lost.

[b] Using the word *wenn* (if) correctly can be difficult to master, but you can learn one or two set phrases like this one to create a good impression. Other examples are *Wenn ich könnte.* (If I could.); *Wenn es möglich wäre.* (If it were possible); *Wenn ich Zeit hätte.* (If I had time.)

[c] Always be ready to spell names or addresses as one of the unprepared questions. It is also a good idea to have a couple of German street names, hotels and names of people ready to use for situations like this, where you have to give imaginary details.

Solutions
Speaking

Conversation A *(page 96)*

1. Was für einen Beruf haben deine Eltern?

    Mein Vater ist leider arbeitslos, aber wenn er arbeitet, ist er Verkäufer in einem Elektrogeschäft. Meine Mutter arbeitet in der Stadtbibliothek.[a]

2. Wie kommen deine Eltern zur Arbeit?

    Meine Mutter geht zu Fuß, weil wir nicht weit von der Stadtmitte wohnen.[b] **Mein Vater fährt normalerweise mit dem Auto.**[c]

3. Hast du einen Job am Wochenende?

    Nein, aber sofort nach dem Examen werde ich mit einem Job in einem großen Kaufhaus in der Stadtmitte anfangen.[d]

4. Was möchtest du nach der Schule machen?

    Ich gehe auf die Fachhochschule hier in der Stadt, um Sportwissenschaft zu studieren, wenn ich gute Noten kriege.[e]

[a] This is a variation on the *Nein, aber ...* idea and here it gives the opportunity to keep the answer going. You need to prepare carefully how to describe your parents' jobs. *GCSE German Vocabulary* has many suggestions. In this case you could also say *Er kann keine Stelle finden.* (He can't find a job.); *Es ist nicht einfach, so eine Stelle zu finden.* (It isn't easy to find such a job.) If you cannot find out the name of the job, you should say the place where they work. For example, *Meine Mutter arbeitet bei Jones and Barker, im Büro.* (My mother works at Jones and Barker's in the office.); *Mein Vater hat eine Stelle in einer Bank. Ich weiß nicht genau, was er macht.* (My father has a job in a bank, I don't know exactly what he does.)

[b] A good use of a *weil*-clause to add extra information.

[c] You could add here *Die Fahrt dauert etwa zwanzig Minuten.* (The journey lasts about twenty minutes.)

[d] Again, a good *Nein, aber ...* sentence, particularly impressive because of the future tense which follows.

[e] You may want to talk about staying at school and say what subjects you plan to study: *Ich hoffe, in die Oberstufe zu gehen, wenn ich gute Noten kriege, um Theater, Englisch und Deutsch zu lernen.* (I hope to go into the sixth form, if I get good marks, to study Drama, English and German.).

Conversation B *(page 96)*

1. Was mußt du machen, um dein Geld zu verdienen?

    Also, da ich keinen Job habe, bekomme ich fünf Pfund die Woche von meinen Eltern. Dafür muß ich mein Zimmer putzen, das Auto waschen und den Tisch decken.[a]

2. Möchtest du Lehrer werden?

    Ja, ich möchte vielleicht Sportlehrer werden.[b]

    Warum?

    Ich treibe sehr gern Sport und ich finde, daß unsere Sportlehrer viel Spaß an ihrer Arbeit haben.

3. Was hast du als Betriebspraktikum gemacht?

    Ach, das war wirklich toll. Ich habe in einem privaten Sportklub gearbeitet. Sie hatten alle möglichen Fitnessgeräte und ein schönes, beheiztes Schwimmbad. Nach meiner Arbeit durfte ich alles benutzen, Schwimmbad, Sauna, alles. Ich war sehr traurig, als mein Praktikum zu Ende war.[c]

[a] You could add an opinion here, such as *Meine Eltern sind wirklich gemein, finde ich. Meine Freunde bekommen Taschengeld für nichts!* (My parents are really mean, I think. My friends get pocket-money for nothing!)

[b] If you want to give the opposite answer you might say *Nein, überhaupt nicht! Ich hasse die Schule, ich will nicht mein ganzes Leben hier verbringen!* (No, certainly not! I hate school, I don't want to spend my whole life here!).

[c] This answer includes past tenses and opinions and would gain excellent marks. Be sure to prepare a similar one for your work experience. There are other suggestions in some of the rôle-plays above. Remember that you don't have to tell the truth in your oral exam. If you prefer you can use your imagination to say interesting things which you have learnt to say correctly and which you know will score highly.

Solutions
Speaking

4 Was sind die Vor- und Nachteile von dieser Arbeit?

Wie gesagt,ᵈ man darf alles selbst benutzen, aber die Leute sind auch sehr freundlich und haben mir viel geholfen. Ich habe viel gelernt. Was manchmal schwer ist, ist bis zehn Uhr abends zu arbeiten. Ich würde lieber als Sportlehrer arbeiten, dann hat man den Abend frei.ᵉ

d This is a neat phrase to introduce a repetition of information (As I said …).

e Here again, we have an answer including past tenses and an opinion. Other useful phrases include: *Es war langweilig, weil ich nicht viel zu tun hatte.* (It was boring because I didn't have much to do.); *Die Leute waren unsympathisch.* (The people weren't nice); *Die Arbeit war sehr schwer und ich war sehr müde am Abend.* (The work was very hard and I was very tired in the evening.); *Ich würde sehr gerne so eine Stelle haben, wenn ich die Schule verlasse.* (I would really like a job like that when I leave school.)

Area E

1
Rôle-play *(page 97)*

Lehrer(in): Sie sind in einer Wechselstube. Ich bin der Angestellte.

Kann ich Ihnen helfen?

Du: Ja, ich möchte zwanzig Pfund in Schilling wechseln.

Lehrer(in): Haben Sie Reiseschecks?

Du: Nein, zwei Zehnpfundscheine.

Lehrer(in): Danke schön. Also, das macht 315 Schilling.

Du: Haben Sie Fünfschillingstücke, bitte?

Lehrer(in): Moment mal. Ja, ich gebe Ihnen fünf Fünfschillingstücke, geht das?

Du: Ja, danke, das geht.

2
Rôle-play A *(page 98)*

Lehrer(in): Sie sind in einem Verkehrsamt in Österreich. Ich bin der Mann im Büro.

Wie kann ich Ihnen helfen?

Du: Ich fahre nächste Wocheᵃ nach Deutschland und möchte Auskunft, bitte.

Lehrer(in): Wo genau möchten Sie hinfahren?

Du: In den Schwarzwald.ᵇ Ich glaube, daß es sehr schön dort ist.ᶜ

Lehrer(in): Ja, sicher. Hier ist eine Broschüre für Sie. Wie wollen Sie hinfahren?

Du: Mit dem Zug. Ich habe eine Studentenkarte, weil ich lieber mit dem Zug als mit dem Bus fahre.ᵈ

Lehrer(in): Gut. Wo wollen Sie wohnen?

Du: In einem Hotel.ᵉ Haben Sie eine Liste? Ich suche etwas nicht zu Teures.

a You could choose any time in the near future: *morgen* (tomorrow), *übermorgen* (the day after tomorrow), *am Montag/Mittwoch* (on Monday/Wednesday).

b You have a free choice of where to go: *nach Köln/Berlin/München/Bayern/in die Alpen* (to Cologne/Berlin/Munich/Bavaria/to the Alps). Be sure you learn some well-known German towns and regions. To be even surer, learn some Austrian and Swiss ones. Can you place *Wien, Zürich, Luzern, Salzburg, Genf, Bern*?

c A good opinion used here. It's sure to score well.

d Another good opinion used with a comparison too.

e You could have chosen *in einer Jugendherberge* (in a youth hostel) or *auf einem Campingplatz* (on a campsite).

142

Lehrer(in):	Das ist eine Liste von allen Hotels im Schwarzwald. Wie lange wollen Sie bleiben?
Du:	**Vielleicht eine Woche, wenn das Wetter schön bleibt.**[f] **Was sind die Freizeitangebote in der Gegend?**
Lehrer(in):	Was machen Sie gern?
Du:	**Ich fahre gern Rad, wandere, schwimme, spiele Tennis.**[g]
Lehrer(in):	Ach, das ist kein Problem. Sport kann man im Schwarzwald sehr gut treiben. Nehmen Sie eine Broschüre mit.
Du:	**Danke schön.**
Lehrer(in):	Nichts zu danken. Gute Reise!

[f] A good reference to the future, using *wenn* (if) to make a condition about how long you stay.

[g] You can use any pastimes you like here: *Ich reite gern/Ich gehe gern spazieren/Ich gehe gern in die Disko/ Ich besichtige Museen und Ruinen/ Ich gehe gern einkaufen/ Ich höre gern Musik und gehe oft in Konzerte* (I like riding/walking/going to the disco/visiting museums and ruins/going shopping/listening to music and I often go to the concerts).

Rôle-play B *(page 99)*

Du:	**Ich möchte Ihnen von meiner Reise mit der Schule nach Frankfurt erzählen.**
Lehrer(in):	Schön. Wann seid ihr gefahren?
Du:	**Es war letztes Jahr am vierzehnten Juli. Wir sind um Mitternacht mit dem Bus von der Schule abgefahren. Es war wirklich aufregend, mitten in der Nacht abzufahren, anstatt ins Bett zu gehen!**
Lehrer(in):	Und habt ihr gar nicht geschlafen?
Du:	**Nein, überhaupt nicht. Wir haben Musik gehört, Karten gespielt und viel geplaudert. Niemand war müde, außer vielleicht den Lehrern!**
Lehrer(in):	Ja, du hast Recht! Wann seid ihr angekommen?
Du:	**Wir mußten erst um halb neun vom Victoria-Bahnhof mit dem Zug abfahren, und so hatten wir Zeit, unterwegs Pause zu machen, um zur Toilette zu gehen oder eine Tasse Kaffee zu trinken.**
Lehrer(in):	Warst du nicht sehr müde nach der Reise im Bus?
Du:	**Ja, ich muß zugeben, daß ich in London ein bißchen schläfrig war. Dann haben wir in einem vornehmen Hotel gefrühstückt – das war toll. Nachher im Zug nach Dover haben wir gesungen und sind schon bald angekommen.**
Lehrer(in):	Wie war die Überfahrt nach Belgien?
Du:	**Schrecklich. Es war furchtbar stürmisch, und viele von meinen Freunden waren seekrank. Ich aber nicht, ich hatte Tabletten gegen Seekrankheit genommen. Übrigens sind wir glücklicherweise nicht nach Belgien gefahren, sondern nach Frankreich, und die Reise war viel schneller vorbei. Das nächste Mal fahre ich durch den Tunnel, das ist noch schneller, und man wird nicht seekrank!**
Lehrer(in):	Das ist eine gute Idee. Wo seid ihr in Frankreich ausgestiegen?
Du:	**Es war in Calais, um zwölf Uhr fünfundzwanzig. Dann sind wir mit dem Zug weitergefahren. Dann waren wir alle müde und haben ein bißchen geschlafen. Wir hatten auch Zeitschriften dabei und haben auch ab und zu gelesen.**

Solutions
Speaking

Lehrer(in): Ist der Zug direkt nach Frankfurt gefahren?

Du: Nein, wir mußten in Köln umsteigen. Wir haben den berühmten Kölner Dom und den Rhein vom Zug gesehen, hatten aber keine Zeit, die Stadt zu besichtigen. Ich würde gern nächstes Jahr Köln und das Rheinland besuchen. Ich werde mit meinen Freunden in Deutschland zelten oder in Jugendherbergen wohnen.

Lehrer(in): Toll! Aber wann seid ihr endlich in Frankfurt angekommen?

Du: Um zwanzig nach sieben sind wir am Hauptbahnhof Frankfurt angekommen. Am Ausgang warteten alle Gastfamilien. Wir waren sehr begeistert, unser erste Besuch in Deutschland! Meine deutsche Familie, Familie Springer, war sehr nett. Sie haben einen grossen Mercedes und wohnen in einem sehr schönen Haus am Stadtrand. Als wir zu Hause waren, war ich so müde, daß ich fast sofort ins Bett gehen wollte.

Lehrer(in): Hoffentlich hast du Spaß bei der Familie Springer gehabt.

Du: Ja, viel Spaß. Mein Partner, Jens, ist sehr sympathisch, wir haben uns gut angefreundet. Nach dem Examen fahre ich alleine nach Frankfurt, um drei Wochen bei Jens zu wohnen. Diesmal nehme ich aber das Flugzeug!

3
Rôle-play C *(page 102)*

Lehrer(in): Guten Abend. Kann ich Ihnen helfen?

Du: Guten Abend. Ich möchte ein Einzelzimmer für heute abend, bitte.

Lehrer(in): Haben Sie eine Reservierung?

Du: Nein, ich habe keine Reservierung.

Lehrer(in): Und was für ein Zimmer wollen Sie?

Du: Ein Einzelzimmer mit Dusche, bitte.

Lehrer(in): Und wie lange wollen Sie bleiben?

Du: Nur eine Nacht.

Lehrer(in): Also, wir haben ein Einzelzimmer mit Bad im dritten Stock. Geht das?

Du: Ja, ich nehme es.

Lehrer(in): Gut. Ihr Name, bitte.

Du: Johnson.

Lehrer(in): Und wie schreibt man das, bitte?

Du: J O H N S O N. Wo kann ich hier essen?

Lehrer(in): Wir haben leider kein Restaurant im Hotel.

Du: Gibt es ein Restaurant hier in der Nähe?

Lehrer(in): Ja, es gibt ein gutes Restaurant etwa zweihundert Meter von hier.

Du: Vielen Dank. Gute Nacht.